Buzz Doering k ... everything you've wanted to know—but didn't know you wanted to know—about leasing. In *The BUZZ on Leasing*, he lets his readers in on all of it.

If you've never leased a car, you will at the very least wonder whether you should have. And whether you will the next time.

If you're planning to lease a car, this is an indispensable guide. When you find the right car and the right dealer or leasing company, this book will guide you through the leasing process.

You'll be able to ask the right questions and recognize the right answers. And if you happen upon the wrong dealer, you'll be able to spot a bad deal before your name goes on the dotted line.

Buzz Doering teaches his readers the basic economics of leasing, including everything from tax advantages to manufacturers' subsidies. And his simple and direct writing unravels complexities and clears up confusion.

Don't go into a dealership without this book.

THE
BUZZ
ON
LEASING

To Geoff,

with best

Regards!

CHRISTMAS

2002

Buzz

THE BUZZ ON LEASING

Should You Lease Your Next Vehicle?

Buzz Doering

B

Jameson Books, Inc.
Ottawa, Illinois

Jameson books are available at special discounts for bulk purchases for sales promotions, premiums, fund raising or educational use. Special condensed or excerpted paperback editions can also be created to customer specifications.

For information or other requests please write:

Jameson Books, Inc.
722 Columbus Street
Ottawa, Illinois 61350
815-434-7905 • FAX 815-434-7907
E-mail 72557.3635@compuserve.com

Book design by Catherine E. Campaigne

Jameson Books titles are distributed to the book trade by LPC Group, 1436 West Randolph Street, Chicago, IL 60607. Bookstores should call 800-243-0138.

Individuals who wish to order by mail should call 800-426-1357.

ISBN 0-915463-79-2
Manufactured in the United States of America
First Printing January 1998

1   2   3   4 / 00   99   98

Contents

- Protect your assets
- GAP protection
- Tax benefits of leasing

- Higher customer retention
- Good used cars
- Increasing sales and service
- Leasing and dealer profits

- Don't get burned
- What to look for in a lease
- The Federal Truth in Leasing Act
- How to judge whether you're getting a good deal

- Independent lease companies
- Leasing frees up time and money
- Easier budgeting and off-balance-sheet financing
- The 1986 Tax Reform Act

INTRODUCTION

THE VEHICLE-LEASING BUSINESS HAS GROWN tremendously over the last 20 years, and especially in the last five. In 1996, 34 percent of the vehicles delivered to consumers were leased, a 10-percent increase over the year before—and it is estimated that the 1997 lease market will exceed 36 percent. The primary reason for this tremendous growth in leasing is that peoples' wages have not keep pace with the price of vehicles. Between 1985 and 1995 the price of vehicles increased 70 percent while wages went up only 35 percent. Leasing enables people to afford the vehicles they want.

Vehicle leasing is probably the most misunderstood consumer transaction. My extensive research for automobile manufacturers and finance companies clearly shows that among non-lessees the lease-literacy rate in America is about 2 percent. My research has taught me about the public's attitude toward leasing, and I know where that attitude comes from. What's more, I know that this lack of knowledge on the part of consumers contributes to the many consumer abuses that give leasing a bad name.

This book was written to explain to consumers how leasing actually works, to address the most common misconceptions about leasing, to point out many potential pitfalls, and to help readers decide for themselves whether to lease or buy their next vehicles. It will show those who do decide to lease what type of lease to look for and how to avoid being taken advantage of by the dealer.

This book will not only help new lessees, but it will also help people who have already leased a vehicle. In my research I found that even people who have entered into lease agreements frequently have no idea what they have done; whether or not they got a fair deal; or what their rights, obligations, and options are during and at the end of the lease.

This book, therefore, is for anyone who's in the market for a vehicle in the next two years and for anyone who's either bought or leased a vehicle in the past year. The information here is not biased for or against leasing, because leasing is not better or worse than buying—it is different from buying. The facts contained here put consumers in a better position to judge whether or not leasing makes sense for them.

Finally, this book addresses the two major lease markets—consumer and commercial. It does not deal with the car rental business (Hertz, Avis, Budget).

Chapter One

The Most Common Misperceptions About Leasing

EASING, AS I SAID IN MY INTRODUCTION, IS THE most misunderstood consumer transaction. Very few people understand how it works or are aware of its pros and cons. Newspaper and television consumer reporters often reflect this lack of knowledge and confusion about leasing.

Leasing isn't for everybody, but when consumers have leases explained to them, when they really understand leasing, and when leases are tailored to their needs, they very often find that leasing a vehicle is to their advantage.

Most people approach leasing , however, with a number of inaccurate ideas about it.

Leasing is not renting

The vast majority of people don't know the difference between leasing a car and renting one, say, from Hertz or

Avis. In fact, many people use the words interchangeably—
"I want to **rent** a car for three years" or "I want to **lease** a
car for the weekend"—as if the two words were synonyms.

Leasing is totally different from renting, but you can't
blame the general public for this confusion. Look in the
Yellow Pages under *Automobiles* and you are likely to find
a heading like "Lease/Rental." And when you *rent* an
apartment, you sign a *lease.* But when it comes to vehicles, the two words do *not* mean the same thing.

What happens when you rent a car?

- You pay very high rates for your use of the vehicle.
- You get a used vehicle that may be dirty (cigarette
  butts in the ash tray, etc.).
- You get very little choice of the vehicle you'll drive.
- You typically have the vehicle for a short time (a
  day, week, or at most a month).
- You have no right to buy the car at the end of the
  rental period.

Leasing is entirely different.
What happens when you lease a car?

- Your payment is far less expensive because you pay
  only for the part of the car you use.
- You get a brand new car with zero miles (and a
  clean ashtray).
- You get to choose the make, model, color, and
  equipment.

- You typically keep the leased car for as long as you would if you'd bought it—two, three, or four years.
- You have the right to buy the car, usually at a fixed price, at the end of the lease.

A few years ago I gave an interview to the automotive editor of a national publication. He began by saying that leasing was essentially the same as renting, so I spent most of the interview, explaining the differences to him. The article that appeared was pretty well balanced, but I wonder what he would have written if I hadn't had the opportunity to educate him.

Leasing really is an educational process. Most of the customers I've leased to in my career were initially opposed to the idea. What changed their minds was that educational process. I didn't trick them or even "sell" them on leasing. They simply *wanted* to lease after they'd been educated! And, of course, I put them into leases tailored to their individual needs.

It makes perfect sense that people want to own their vehicles. After all, they think, why make all those payments and have nothing to show for them at the end? They equate it with renting a home. Renters pay a landlord, and often the property they are renting goes up in value. So the rent goes up as well. When the renters move out, who gets the profit? The landlord! The renter has nothing to show but a bunch of canceled checks. But comparing renting an apartment to leasing a vehicle isn't valid.

Why not? *Because vehicles don't go* up *in value while you are driving them—they go* down *in value!* So, if you want to know where your $300-per-month payment goes, it goes to cover the vehicle's depreciation while you are driving it. You start with a $24,000 vehicle and drive it while it declines in value to $12,000. That's why John Paul Getty is quoted as saying that you should buy appreciating assets, but you should lease depreciating assets.

What about equity at the end of the lease? Well, compare the cost of the lease to the cost of buying and financing the same vehicle over the same period of time. The lessee has saved money. He might not have equity in the vehicle, but he has cash he can use to buy the vehicle at the end of the lease. Of course, he doesn't have to buy it if he doesn't want to, and he doesn't have to make up his mind until the end of the lease when he's in a better position to judge whether it is a good vehicle and a good deal.

The equity in a lease is cash

When you purchase a vehicle and finance it, your payment covers three things—the vehicle's depreciation, the interest, and an equity contribution. You actually gain equity, because when the loan has been paid down to zero, the vehicle still has value ($10,000 to $12,000). Does it make sense to drive around for three years with thousands of dollars in cash in your glove compartment? If not, why would you drive around with thousands of dollars' worth of equity in your vehicle?

In order to have equity in a vehicle you're financing, you must be paying more per month than is really necessary. This means that if you *have* equity in a vehicle, you're overpaying for it. If you *don't have* equity in a vehicle, you have a lower monthly payment. Equity doesn't appear miraculously—it comes directly out of your pocket!

But what if you pay cash for a car? Isn't that better than leasing? Not necessarily. The "one-payment leases" now available are ideal for the cash buyer. Leasing's biggest advantage for a cash buyer is that it removes the risk of depreciation. The purchase price of a car is not your cost. Your cost is the difference between the purchase price and what you can eventually sell it—or trade it in—for at the end of the term. That is called depreciation. Why pay for the whole car when you can pay for only the part you are using? You have no idea and no control over what that depreciation will be until you sell the vehicle. I tell cash buyers that leasing is an insurance policy, a way to insure the future value of their asset, a way to insure their transportation costs. When was the last time you went to Las Vegas and gambled $5000 on a single bet? You take a very similar gamble when you pay cash for a car. On the other hand, the customer gives up nothing when she leases—all she does is gain.

You never give up the right of ownership

What if you usually keep a car for an extended period of time, say seven or eight years? Will leasing still work for you? Well, it won't if you aren't given a fixed option to buy the vehicle at the end of the lease. *Today most leases are written with that option at the end,* so the customer can lease for three years and—if nothing changes—he can then buy the vehicle with the money he's saved and keep it as long as he likes. It's the best of leasing and the best of ownership.

But things do change! For instance, you might change jobs or move. Your family might get bigger—or smaller. Automobile manufacturers might come out with some new technology or some new safety features. Three years from now we might have a car that gets 75 miles to a gallon of gas. Or the change might be in your car itself: maybe you've had an accident and the car's been badly damaged. It's been repaired, but you don't want it any more. If, for *any* reason, you don't want your leased vehicle after the three years are up, just give it back and the lease company suffers the extra depreciation on the wrecked-and-repaired car or deals with the fact that new technology makes this car outdated. If you've *bought* it and you want to get rid of it after three years, will you be able to sell it? Will you be able to sell it for the same amount of cash you'd have saved by leasing?

In leasing you never give up the right of ownership. You just postpone the day you have to make the decision.

High-mileage drivers save by leasing

The conventional wisdom is that, if you drive more than 15,000 miles per year, leasing won't work for you because leases include mileage limits, and there's a big penalty for exceeding the limit. Most articles on leasing support that belief. But the "wisdom" is wrong!

The high-mileage driver actually benefits even *more* from leasing. She can build the extra miles she needs into the lease (for about 8 to 10 cents a mile), or she can pay for the extra miles at the end of the lease (for about 10 to 15 cents per mile).

Why is this a good deal? Because the used-car wholesale guide books depreciate high-mileage cars at about 20 cents per mile. That means that high-mileage drivers can buy the miles they need more cheaply from the lease company than from themselves. The more miles the customer drives, the more money she saves!

There's no 15,000-mile-per-year limit in leasing, and there's no penalty at the end. Here is how it works. The first 15,000 miles on a leased car are free. Any miles over and above that cost the customers 8 to 15 cents each depending on when they pay for them. That isn't a mileage penalty. It's a vehicle-usage charge. Penalties are applied when someone has done something wrong. A vehicle-usage charge simply requires the customer to pay for the extra depreciation caused by driving those extra miles. In addition, very few people realize that, if the customer buys the vehicle at the end or trades out prematurely, the vehicle-usage charge is never imposed. A customer who buys the car at the end of the lease is in exactly the same ownership position as a customer who buys the vehicle in the first place.

It is unfortunate that most consumer writers do not understand this mileage issue. They typically advise any driver who travels 30,000 miles a year to buy his vehicle instead of leasing it. The consumer would probably finance the car for 60 months, then try to trade out of it after 36 months. When the car is appraised with 90,000 miles on it, it will be worth substantially less than is owed to the bank. The customer will have to come up with thousands of dollars to trade the vehicle. Lacking the cash, this customer often ends up adding the deficit to his next loan and piling interest on top of it! In such a case, buying the vehicle would cost the consumer *far* more than leasing it.

CHAPTER TWO

How a Lease Works

IN SOME RESPECTS, THE PROCESS OF LEASING A VEHICLE is the same as the process of purchasing one. You do your research and choose the vehicle that suits your needs and your budget. Whether you go to a dealer or to an independent leasing company, you get to choose the make, model, color, and options. If you decide to lease a new vehicle, you will get a brand new car with no miles on its odometer—just as you would if you bought a new vehicle. Leasing is a financial transaction. The difference between leasing and buying is not in the vehicle but in how the financing is handled.

How the payment is figured

When you lease, your monthly payment is determined by two main factors: the **depreciation** over the period of usage and the **lease charges.** *Lease charges* are sometimes referred to as finance charges, rental charges, or interest. In fact, they compensate the lease company for the economic use value of the asset (the car).

Depreciation is the loss in the value of the vehicle between the time the lessee drives it away and the end of the lease. To determine depreciation, the lease company starts with the capitalized cost—the initial value of the vehicle as shown on the face of the consumer lease. This amount might be the Manufacturer's Suggested Retail Price (MSRP, or window sticker), but it might also be more or less, depending on market demand for that particular vehicle. Once the initial value is set, the lease company will establish the residual, the amount the lease company thinks the vehicle will be worth on the wholesale market at the end of the lease. Typically, most lease companies offer closed-end leases which make the lease company—not the consumer—responsible for the residual at the end of the lease.

The residual is subtracted from the capitalized cost, and the difference between the two is the total depreciation. To calculate monthly depreciation, you simply divide the total depreciation by the number of months in the lease.

The "24 Rule"

The lease charges are figured in one of two ways: some lease companies equate them with an interest percentage, and others use a "money factor." There is very little difference between the two because in both cases lease charges are based on the average outstanding value of the leased vehicle. However, using a "money factor" is a shortcut. You can easily convert lease-rate percentages to a "money factor" and vice versa by using the "24 Rule." The "24 Rule" applies to all leases, regardless of dollar amount or length of lease. To convert a lease rate percentage to a "money factor," *divide* by 24 and carry the decimal. To convert a "money factor" to a percentage, *multiply* by 24 and carry the decimal.

EXAMPLE

A 7.2% lease rate divided by 24 = a "money factor" of .003.
A "money factor" of .003 $\times$ 24 = a 7.2% lease rate.

The lease charge is based on the average outstanding value of the vehicle leased. Average outstanding value is the value of the vehicle at the mid-point of the lease, and it is computed by averaging the capitalized cost and the residual. Add the two and divide by two. The monthly lease charge is calculated on that amount.

EXAMPLE

The capitalized cost is $24,000 and the residual is $14,400.
Add the two for a total of $38,400.
Divide by two for an average outstanding balance of $19,200.

If the lease rate is presented as an annual percentage, say, of 7.2%, divide 7.2% by 12 (months per year) and you get a monthly lease rate of .6%. Multiply the .6% by the average outstanding balance of $19,200 and that gives you a monthly lease charge of $115.20.

Using the "money factor" to calculate lease charges is a little different. Now you add the capitalized cost and the residual and multiply that sum by the "money factor." Add the $24,000 capitalized cost to the $14,400 residual, for a total of $38,400. Multiply the $38,400 total by the "money factor" of .003 and you get the same monthly lease charge of $115.20.

To get the total lease charges, multiply the monthly lease charge by the number of months. As you can see, whether you use a lease rate or a money factor, two identical vehicles leased for the same length of time at the same rate will have the same monthly lease charges.

Sometimes people ask why, when a "money factor" is used, it is multiplied by the capitalized cost *plus* the residual? Isn't the consumer paying too much interest? **NO!** Using the "24 Rule" of conversion compensates for that. The lease rate is cut in half and then divided by 12 to give you the "money factor."

EXAMPLE

A 7.2% lease rate converted to a monthly "money factor" is
$$7.2\% \div (2 \times 12) = .003$$

"Money factors" are nothing more than shortcuts and time savers. Once the monthly depreciation and monthly lease charges are calculated, they are added and that total is your basic monthly payment.

Look at this example of a 36-month lease:

Capitalized cost $24,000
Residual @ 60% $-14,400$
Total Depreciation $ 9,600 ÷ 36 months
= $266.66 Monthly Depreciation

Lease charges at a 7.2% lease rate divided by 24 equals a .003 "money factor."

Capitalized cost $24,000
Residual @ 60% +14,400
$38,400 × .003
= $115.20 Monthly Lease Charges

Monthly Depreciation $266.66
Monthly Lease Charges $115.20
Basic Lease Payment $381.86

What are lease rates?

The remark that by leasing you pay only for the part of the car you use refers to depreciation. That is why lease payments are always lower than finance payments. Often, people are led to believe that in a lease no interest is charged on the residual. That is not the case. Interest *is* charged on the whole vehicle—and it should be. After all, the consumer who leases has the use of the whole vehicle. In fact, if you compare a lease to a loan on the same vehicle over the same period, the total interest on the lease will be more than the total interest on the loan. Why? Because the average outstanding balance on the lease is higher than on the loan. The lease pays down only to the residual, and the loan pays down to zero. The customer can compensate for this difference, however, by investing the money he saves by leasing at the same (or an even better!) rate of return as that used to calculate his lease payment. In such a case, the customer's net interest cost on the lease would be the same as on a loan.

The most common lease today is the closed-end lease with a fixed option at the end, sometimes referred to as a *net lease* or a *walk-away lease*. Once the consumer completes the agreed monthly payments, he has **four options:**

1. If the customer likes the vehicle and wants to continue driving it, he **may purchase it** for the fixed option. This amount is decided up front and put in writing in the contract. The amount represents the part of the car the consumer didn't pay for in the lease. By paying this sum, he simply completes the sale. He can use the money he saved through making lower payments. If he has spent the money or has invested it and doesn't want to liquidate his investment, most lease companies will offer either an extension of the lease or financing. So, if the customer wants to keep the vehicle at the end of the lease but he can't

come up with the money to buy it, there is no worry that it will be taken away.

2. The customer may simply **return the car to the lease company** at the end of the lease. If he hasn't driven more than the allowed miles and the vehicle has not been abused, the customer has no further obligation. If the market value of the vehicle turns out to be less than the residual, the leasing company takes the loss. The company absorbs part of the vehicle's depreciation, thus paying part of the customer's transportation costs. It is not unusual for an off-lease vehicle to be worth far less than the residual.

3. If the customer doesn't want to buy the car, he can get it appraised to find out its value (this can be done at any new- or used-car dealer). If it is worth more than his residual, he can exercise his option to **buy it, then sell it for the higher amount and keep the profit.** This has been common practice in the last few years with sport utility vehicles and trucks. Keep in mind, however, that when a customer does decide to buy his off-lease vehicle, he may be required to pay a state sales tax, and that, of course, lowers his profit.

4. After the customer has his vehicle appraised and finds that it is worth more than his buyout (i.e., he has equity in it), he may **use it as a trade-in** on his next vehicle. The equity can either be given

back in the form of a check or be subtracted from the price of the next vehicle. In some states this eliminates the need to pay sales tax on the buy-out price.

The **residual** that the leasing company uses is a major factor in determining your monthly payment. If this residual is unrealistically high, your payment will be lower. If the vehicle is sold for less than the residual, the lease company absorbs the loss and you get the benefit of an unrealistically low payment. But, if the residual is *too* low, it will drive the payment higher. Nevertheless, you have the right to buy the vehicle at the end of the lease for the lower residual and sell it for the higher market value. Your profit on the sale makes up for the higher payments you made. In effect, you get back what you were overcharged.

That is why I advise customers not to worry too much about the residual used to calculate their payments. If the residual is too high, let the lease company absorb the loss. If the residual is too low, keep the profit at the end. Leasing removes the risk of depreciation by telling you up front what your depreciation will be. That makes leasing ideal for conservative people who don't like risk and for people on a fixed income or budget. They know ahead of time exactly what their transportation costs will be. It takes the gamble out of the used-car market.

Other fees and factors

Many lease companies also charge an **acquisition fee**—usually $300 to $500—for writing the lease. Sometimes it is paid by the customer up front, but usually it is built into the lease and added to the monthly payment at about $10 per month. It is an additional fee paid to the leasing company in much the same way that you pay "points" to a bank when you take out a mortgage. It covers the credit check, documentation, and paper work. Because the acquisition fee skews the annual percentage rate, you can't refer to lease rates as simple interest or as an annual percentage rate. As part of the overall profit picture for the leasing company reflected in the lease rate, the acquisition fee is usually not negotiable.

There are three more major factors in developing a lease. The first is **term.** How long will the lease contract be? My answer to that is, "How long do you plan to keep the vehicle?" Lease it for your expected period of usage. True, the longer the lease, the lower the payment. But it's a mistake to lease a car for too long just to get a lower payment. If you want to get out of the lease before the end, you have to make up the difference between the lease payoff and the market value of the vehicle. At that point, you will have to pay the amount that the vehicle has depreciated over what you've already paid. It could be thousands of dollars!

This practice was a major contributor to leasing's bad reputation. In the late 1980s many consumers, tempted by low payments, got into leases that were too long. When they tried to get out of these leases early, they got a very rude awakening. They either had to come up with thousands of dollars or keep the vehicles and pay the higher maintenance that you expect as a vehicle ages. Always remember that, though a short-term lease payment is higher, you can walk away at the end of the lease. Plus, in most cases, the shorter the lease term, the lower the lease rate. Wouldn't you rather pay for something over the time you use it than be charged a big amount when the contract is over? Most leases are for two, three, or four years.

The second major consideration is **how many miles** you will be driving during this lease. As I explained in chapter 1, most leases allow 15,000 miles per year and charge 8 to 15 cents per mile over that. You can add the mileage fee to the monthly payment or pay it at the end of the lease. If you bought the same vehicle and drove the same number of miles, you'd find at trade-in time that your car had depreciated in value about 20 cents per mile for those extra miles. Leasing, then, saves you 5 to 12 cents a mile, and the more miles you drive, the more money you save by leasing. I usually recommend that customers build the additional mileage charge into the payment. It raises the payment, but at the end of the lease you can walk away with no additional charges. On the other hand, if you are not sure how many miles you will be driving, I *don't* recommend building mileage into the payment. Not all companies will refund the unused mileage payment. If you buy the vehicle at the end of the lease, the extra mileage charge will be subtracted from your buyout. But, if you don't want to keep the vehicle, the only way to get your money back is to buy it at the lower price, then turn around and sell it for a higher price—which may or may not be possible.

Consumers should also ask themselves, "How much money will I have to come up with to start the lease?" In past years too many companies advertised "no money down" leases, then asked the customer for thousands of dollars at delivery time. Technically, there is no down payment on a lease. If there were, it would represent additional profit for the dealer, and the customer would not be given credit for it in the lease. From a practical standpoint, though, the customer may be asked for money up front to start the lease, and that is construed—especially by the customer, who has to write the check—as a down payment. In leasing, this money is called a **"start-up fee."**

Most of the start-up fee is a capitalized cost reduction, more commonly referred to as the **"cap-cost reduction."** In some parts of the country it is called the "de-cap." This is money the customer pays up front, and it is subtracted from the capitalized cost of the vehicle. This part of the transaction must be shown on the front of a consumer lease, and it lowers the monthly lease payment. For example, if the cap-cost reduction is $3600 on a 36 month lease, the lease payment will be reduced by $100 per month plus interest savings. Many lease companies advertise very low lease payments, but the fine print calls for big cap-cost reductions. To me, this neutralizes one of the major benefits of leasing. There are better things to do with your money than tie it up in a vehicle. Theoretically, you could offer a $20,000 vehicle for a $5 per month lease payment with a $19,900 cap-cost reduction!

Most leases require a **security deposit** and the **first-month lease payment** up front. The security deposit is refunded at the end of the lease if the consumer fulfills her obligations. Sometimes the security deposit and first-month lease payment are built into the lease. In that case, the customer doesn't have to pay these amounts up front, but they will be reflected in her higher monthly payments.

Finally, bear in mind that sometimes there are up-front **license and title fees, and taxes.** These vary depending on the state or province. Some lease companies charge the license and title fees up front, while others build them into the payment. Some states collect sales tax up front and others add it to the monthly payment without adding interest. Some states have excise or property taxes that are either paid up front or added to the payment. You will be expected to pay license and title fees and property tax either directly up front or indirectly in your lease payments even though you don't own the vehicle.

Leasing a vehicle—from the time you choose the vehicle you want to the time you have the exclusive control of it, including all rights and obligations—is very much the same as buying. In terms of finances and risk, however, leasing is very different. Leasing saves you money that can be spent or invested elsewhere. It also removes the risk factor from the vehicle's depreciation.

To further your understanding of how a lease works, this is a picture of a lease for a $24,000 vehicle. The residual, after 36 months, is 60% of the MSRP, or $14,400.

A picture of a lease

$24,000 VEHICLE

BUY	LEASE
PAY ALL $24,000	PAY $9,600 DEPRECI- ATION
	AT LEASE END
	SAVE $14,400 THE RESIDUAL @ 60%

You have four choices:

1. Buy and keep for $14,400
2. Turn back to lease company
3. Buy at option and sell (if it's worth more than $14,400)
4. Use as trade-in on next vehicle—if it's worth more than $14,400

In the lease, the depreciation is $9600 ÷ 36 = $266.66
In the purchase, the depreciation is $24,000 ÷ 36 = $666.66
The lease depreciation saving is $400.00 per month, or $400 × 36 = $14,400. The same as the residual.

At the end of the lease the customer does not own the vehicle, but he can buy it for the $14,400 he saved while leasing. He doesn't have to make this decision for 36 months (until the end of the lease).

Chapter Three

Which Is More Expensive—Leasing or Buying?

I HAVE BEEN ASKED THIS QUESTION FOR THE 30-PLUS years I have been in the leasing business. I have been asked by friends, clients and strangers, and my answer is always the same: "I don't know!" Usually their response is, "What do you mean you don't know? You have been doing this long enough! *Why* don't you know?" Again, the answer is simple: I can tell you what it costs to lease a vehicle because the depreciation is guaranteed by the leasing company. But I can't tell you what it will cost to own the vehicle until you're ready to sell it. It's just as I explained in chapter 2—the real cost of your vehicle is not what you paid for it. The real cost is the *difference* between what you paid for the vehicle and what you can sell it for. And how can you know that two or three years in advance?

My research for Volkswagen of America and Ford Motor Company shows very clearly that most people think leasing is more expensive than buying—because they don't know the difference between leasing and renting. A few years ago I did a "man on the street" interview in Detroit's business district for Volkswagen of America. The results were hilarious. I stopped people at random and asked, "Have you ever leased a car?" If the answer was yes, I asked whom they leased it from and for how long. I have a video clip of the answers I got: "From Hertz, for a weekend"; "From Avis, on our vacation"; "From Enterprise, for a month while my car was in the body shop." As a matter of fact, when I interviewed a New York agent for this book, he told me that his only experience with leasing was when he went to Europe and leased a car for a week! When people confuse leasing with renting, they naturally assume that leasing is very expensive because they *know* how expensive renting is. Renting a car from Hertz for a month would cost about $1200! People frequently say that leasing would not benefit them because they don't use their cars for business and so can't take their costs as tax write-offs. Convinced that leasing is more expensive than buying, they suppose that they could justify leasing only if they could take it as a deduction on their taxes. Actually, the cash outlay for a lease is less than for a purchase, because a residual is used to calculate the payment. In any given period of time you will pay less on a lease because you pay for only part of the vehicle. So I can tell customers that they'll put out less cash for a lease than for a purchase, but I can't tell them what their ultimate cost will be until the purchased vehicle is sold.

Comparing leasing to buying

When people try to compare the cost of leasing to the cost of buying, I know that they don't really understand leasing. They think it's just another way to buy a vehicle, just a type of alternative financing. They're right, as far as they go. Leasing *is* alternative financing, but it's much more than that. There are many features and benefits of leasing that you can't get if you buy, so the comparison is apples to oranges. Or, better, Cadillacs to Chevrolets. You don't compare the costs of those cars because they are totally different vehicles.

If a customer is trying to decide whether to lease or to buy, she should understand *all* the differences between the two—not just the price differences. Price and cost are two different things. Price is what you pay. Cost relates to value received—what you get for what you pay. Let me give you an example. You go to the store to buy a pair of tennis shoes for your child. The first pair you see is priced at $10, but the consumer disclosure and your own experience tell you you can expect one month's wear out of those shoes under normal playground conditions. The second pair of shoes is priced at $20, but you can expect four months of wear under normal playground usage. The $10 shoes have a lower **price,** but the $20 shoes have a lower **cost.** *Value* is not determined by what you pay, but by what you get for your money. Most people understand that. They want value for their money. Last year, for instance, 180,000 Cadillacs were sold in America. I'll bet not one person who bought a Cadillac actually thought it was cheaper than a Chevrolet. The Cadillac buyers believed they got value for their money.

I want to educate people to view buying and leasing the same way. Leasing is not just another way to buy a car. It is different from buying in a number of ways, and only when you understand these differences can you judge for yourself whether leasing offers value for you or not.

The equity issue

The first and biggest objection we hear to leasing is that the customer has no equity in the vehicle at the end of the lease. My answer is, "That's the beauty of leasing!" Leasing is *designed* not to give you equity in a vehicle. You pay only for the part of the car you use instead of for the whole car, and that saves you cash. Compare a three-year lease with a three-year finance contract. The lease payment will be 40 to 50 percent lower, which means that leasing can save you $200 to $300 per month in payments. True, you won't have equity in the vehicle, but you will have cash savings. And most people can use cash-in-hand to cover monthly expenses, to invest, or to meet emergencies.

As soon as most people realize that equity in a vehicle causes their monthly payment to go up—that, in fact, they are paying extra for that equity—they ask themselves, "What's so great about having equity in a vehicle when the equity is coming out of my wallet?" If you wouldn't drive around with a bag of cash in the back seat, why would you want to drive around with equity in a vehicle?

When you look at leasing, consider the value of cash flow: what else could you do with your money if you didn't tie it up in a vehicle?

Digging out of your trades

Leasing is also a more flexible way to get a new vehicle. Many people buy new vehicles while they still owe a great deal on the cars they're trading in—in fact, they owe more than the trade-in is worth. We used to call that "upside down" or "buried in their trades," but now we have a more politically correct term. We say these buyers are experiencing "financial inversion."

How did the buyer get in such a disadvantageous position? When he bought his current vehicle, he wanted to keep his payments affordable. To do that, he had to finance the purchase over a considerable period of time—longer than he wanted to keep the car. Now that he wants to trade it in, he owes much more than the car is worth. Can he come up with the cash to cover the negative equity? Frequently, no. So he rolls it into the next loan and adds additional interest on top. Some buyers do this with car after car, digging themselves into deeper and deeper holes, simply to afford the vehicles they want. As I've already pointed out, the price of vehicles has increased 70 percent over the last ten years, but people's wages have increased only 35 percent. This extended financing, however, is *not* the solution. It simply makes matters worse by postponing the day of reckoning.

Leasing can help in two ways. The customer may be so upside-down in the trade that buying a new car is impossible. But leasing one would be possible because lease companies typically advance 10 percent more than the sticker price. This extra advance can help pay off the lien holder of the trade-in. (This extra advance, by the way, is not additional profit for the dealer. It goes to cover the customer's negative equity on the trade-in.) It will raise the lease payment, but it will also give the customer the vehicle she wants. The best part is that, with a short-term lease, the customer will have a paid-up contract at the end, with no deficit to carry on to the next vehicle.

One of the biggest benefits for a customer who is experiencing financial inversion is that leasing shortens the trade cycle, allowing customers to trade more often. The typical 60-month finance payment is about the same as a 36-month lease payment, but at the end of the lease the customer has a paid-up contract. There is no negative equity to carry to the next contract. If the customer keeps his purchased vehicle the whole 60 months of the finance term, it will be out of warranty the last two years. If something breaks, the customer pays for it. Even if nothing breaks, the fourth and fifth years of ownership are when maintenance costs kick in—new tires, a tune up, shocks, brakes, exhaust system, and battery. When you compare shorter-term lease payments to longer-term purchase payments, you must bear these repair and maintenance costs in mind. Leasing makes a shorter trade cycle affordable for the customer and saves on maintenance and repairs.

More for your money

Most people today are interested in expensive, more fully loaded vehicles, but they may have difficulty squeezing the vehicle they want into their budgets. Leasing solves that problem. It allows the consumer to have more car for the money. In fact, given similar terms and the same payment, a lease will get the consumer an $8000 to $10,000 more expensive vehicle. Why? Because of the residual. As a rule of thumb, if you are comparing similar terms and the same payment, the residual the lease company uses is the additional value of the vehicle the consumer will get. It's like stacking the dollar amount of the residual on top of the window sticker price, for the same monthly payment.

The sales tax benefit

In some states, there is an additional benefit to leasing. Ordinarily, when you buy a vehicle, you pay a state sales tax based on the selling price of the vehicle. This tax is either paid up front in cash or financed and added to the monthly payment, thus adding to the interest. When you lease, however, you will pay no sales tax up front at all in certain states because the leasing company is tax exempt when it buys the vehicle. A usage tax is added to the monthly payment, usually at the same rate as the sales tax would be. So how do you benefit? In two ways. First, you pay the tax over a period of time rather than in one lump sum, with no interest added to the sales tax. Second, if you turn the vehicle back to the lease company, you pay no sales tax on the residual. The net effect is that you are taxed only on the part of the vehicle that you used. Depending on the rate of the sales tax in your state and the amount of the residual, your savings could amount to several hundred dollars. Of course, if you buy the vehicle at the end of the lease, you will pay sales tax on the residual, but you'll pay it at the end of the lease instead of at the beginning.

I covered the high-mileage benefit in chapter 1. When you judge the value of a lease, consider how many miles per year you will drive. If you drive more than 15,000 miles per year, each additional mile will cost less in leasing fees than it would cost in depreciation on a vehicle you owned. Lease companies typically charge 8 to 10 cents a mile over 15,000 miles a year. The used-car wholesale guidebooks depreciate high-mileage vehicles at 20 to 30 cents a mile. Obviously, the more miles you drive, the more money you save by leasing. High-mileage cost is probably the most misunderstood aspect of leasing.

Leases, lawsuits, and loans

One rarely recognized benefit of leasing applies particularly to retired people and high-income people. Under the law in most states, the owner of a vehicle—not the driver—is primarily responsible for any damage the vehicle does. Not that the driver can't be sued. She can, but the owner is held primarily responsible. In the case of a leased car, *the leasing company is the owner,* so these companies typically carry huge umbrella liability policies.

How does this benefit a retiree? Usually, when you retire, your earning power ends. You may tend to hoard the nest egg you've accumulated. Clearly, a potential lawsuit is a threat to that security, and leasing reduces your liability. This also holds true for high-income people and for people whose teenagers drive the family car. When I started in the leasing business in the mid-1960s, this particular benefit of leasing never occurred to us. Back then, this wasn't such a "lawsuit-happy" society. Today everyone sues everyone for everything—and usually gets it!

An individual or a business may also benefit from leasing because it can increase their borrowing ability.

When you go to a bank for a loan, the first thing the bank looks at is your balance sheet—your list of assets and liabilities. Accountants don't consider a lease a liability. They refer to leasing as "off-balance-sheet financing," which means that you can give the banker a healthier financial statement and give yourself a better chance of getting the loan.

I want to be very clear on this point: I'm not saying that your lease won't show on your credit report. It will. But a credit report is not the same as a balance sheet. And even in terms of your credit report, a lease payment that is lower than a purchase payment clearly improves your income-to-monthly-obligation ratio. None of this guarantees that you will be approved for a loan, but leasing won't hurt your chances in the way that financing a car might. It's a little like going to church on Sunday. You aren't sure if it will help, but you are pretty sure it won't hurt!

Bill-backs and leasing incentives

Research shows that many people are uncomfortable in the process of buying a new vehicle. The only thing that makes them less comfortable is trading in the vehicle they have. That isn't necessary when you lease. You can just turn the vehicle in with no negotiation and no hassle. When a customer leases, she has total control at trade-in time. If she doesn't like the value placed on the used vehicle at the end of the lease, she gives it back and walks away. If she owns the vehicle, she loses control because she has to accept its market value.

Some consumers worry about "abnormal" wear and tear. Will they be billed for scratches and dents when the lease is up? There are two answers to that question. First, the dealer or leasing company will want to lease you another vehicle, so the last thing it wants to do is irritate you with unreasonable bill-backs. Second, if a vehicle *does* have abnormal wear and tear and the lease company bills it back to the customer, it is no different than if the customer were trading in the same vehicle. In that case, the used-car appraiser would subtract the damages from the appraised value. In effect, then, abnormal wear and tear on a leased car won't improve the customer's situation, but it won't make it worse either. And at least the customer won't have to endure the haggling and hassle that typically go with trading in. It's a lot less stressful.

In the early 1980s automobile manufacturers started to offer rebates to consumers who bought new vehicles. It started with Joe Garagiola for Chrysler Corporation— "Get a car. Get a check"—and it remained a very popular marketing incentive through the '80s and early '90s. In the last four or five years, however, both domestic and import manufacturers have put their marketing dollars into leasing.

They subsidize leasing this way: instead of mailing a rebate check to the consumer, the manufacturer sends a check to the leasing company which uses it to reduce the consumer's lease payment. It's like getting 36 rebates, one a month for three years, in the form of lower monthly payments. These subsidies come in two forms: sometimes the lease charges used to calculate the lease are offset by the manufacturer, and the consumer gets a saving in that area. In other cases the residual used by the lease company is subvented—that is, the manufacturer adds 5 to 10 points to the residual listed in the guidebook for a particular model. That substantially lowers the payment. In fact, it's not uncommon to see $2000 to $3000 subsidies built into leases, giving the consumer the benefit of a $50-to-$100 decrease in monthly payments. The more eager manufacturers are to move a particular model, the more willingly they subsidize the leases, so don't look for much of a subsidy on models that are in high demand and short supply.

How do you decide?

Some of the differences between buying and leasing have monetary value, and some don't. It is up to each individual to determine what's important, what has value: Do you have better ways to use your money than by tying it up in a vehicle? Is peace of mind important to you? Are you uncomfortable with risk? Do you want to reduce your stress? These are all personal decisions. Only your own circumstances and judgment can determine which will "cost" more—leasing or buying.

Don't make the very common mistake of trying to "bottom line" a lease-vs.-buy. I often see people add the down payment on a buy to all their monthly payments, then compare that total to the sum of the lease payments and the residual. They figure that will determine which method is cheaper. It won't, because that comparison doesn't work. **The buy example is a cash flow example** which tells you how much cash has been laid out for the vehicle. Nowhere does it address depreciation or assess what the vehicle will be worth at trade-in time. **The lease example is an expense example,** because the depreciation is guaranteed by the lease company. Many consumers unconsciously lift the guaranteed residual off the lease example and apply it to the buy example, but *the residual is not guaranteed when you buy.* Depreciation is the biggest expense in owning a vehicle, and you have no control over it when you buy. Only through leasing is the depreciation guaranteed.

By now you can see why I say that leasing is an educational process, and why many people—once they understand all its features and benefits—decide to lease.

CHAPTER FOUR

Types of Leases

THERE ARE MANY TYPES OF LEASES. THIS CHAPTER will explain the different leases and the other options available in leasing. I hope it will help you decide which lease and which options are the most appropriate for you.

You must take a totally different approach when you lease a vehicle from that taken when you buy one. All the dealers' costs for a particular model are the same, and what you are pricing and buying is just the vehicle. When you lease, however, that's not so. In that case, what you are pricing and purchasing is the lease, and no two leases are identical.

To begin with, you want to sidestep one very common trap: don't "fall into" a lease simply because it offers the lowest payment. You can always get a lower lease payment on any vehicle by altering the terms and conditions of the lease. *Every person who ever got burned on a lease went for the lowest payment.* If your sole criterion for judging a lease is the payment amount, you might as well buy shoes that don't fit simply because they're the cheapest in the store. Both decisions would have very painful consequences.

Your first priority should be to get a lease developed to meet your needs. Cost will follow.

Closed-end and open-end leases

All leases are either open-end or closed-end. Open-end leases are sometimes called finance leases or, in the language of the Internal Revenue Service, TRAC leases. TRAC stands for Terminal Rental Adjustment Clause. Closed-end leases are sometimes called net leases, or walk-away leases. The only difference between open-end and closed-end leases is who bears the burden of risk for depreciation. In an open-end lease, the customer is liable for the residual at the end. In a closed-end lease, the leasing company is liable.

Many people believe that the option to buy the vehicle at the end of the lease makes it an open-end lease. Wrong! There is a world of difference between *being able to buy* a vehicle at the end and *having to buy* that vehicle. You want to be very clear on this point. There is nothing illegal about an open-end lease, if it is a business lease. If it is a consumer lease, an open-end lease is still legal in most states. The catch is that it isn't really a lease—it is considered a conditional sales contract. In some states, however, balloon note financing is illegal, and an open-end consumer lease can be considered a balloon note—making it illegal in those states.

At one time open-end leasing was often used to exploit customers. A customer with an open-end lease is guaranteeing the residual, and the residual is a major factor in determining monthly payments. Many people were suckered into unrealistically low payments, which left them guaranteeing unrealistically high residuals. When the lease was up and the vehicle was sold for less than the guaranteed residual, the customer had to make up the difference—which could amount to thousands of dollars. Today, under the Federal Truth in Leasing Act, the most a customer can be charged back at the end by a leasing company on an open-end lease (relative to the residual) is three monthly payments. Most big business fleets, however, are on open-end leases because open-end leasing is tailored for business use, for those big fleets and, in some cases, for smaller commercial fleets. Usually, the open-end lease is not good for the individual consumer because there is too much risk of misunderstanding and abuse.

Fixed option price at lease end

In any case, most consumers prefer closed-end leases today, and the best one is a closed-end lease with a fixed option price at the end. Not all closed-end leases include this fixed option price. Some clearly state that the customer has no option to purchase the vehicle. Other leases give what is called a "fair market" option at the end. This is a bit nebulous. Fair market refers to what market? Wholesale or retail? Who decides what's "fair"? Without a fixed option price at the end, a vehicle that is worth more than the residual used to calculate the lease payment becomes a windfall profit for the lease company. In a closed-end lease with a fixed option, the risk of depreciation is on the shoulders of the lease company. If there is a loss at the end, the lease company absorbs it; but if there is a gain at the end, the customer gets it. It's a win-win situation for the customer: the profit opportunity at the end of the lease is unlimited, but the downside risk is zero. Think about it. Where does the consumer get a better deal? Usually wherever there is profit potential, there is risk of loss. Not in leasing. A consumer in a closed-end lease with a fixed option price will win regardless of the vehicle's value at the end of the lease. That's why I tell customers not to worry about the residual the lease company uses. If it turns out to be too high, the lease company eats the loss. If it turns out to be too low, the customer can buy the vehicle at the lower residual. Then he can turn around and sell it for a profit or use it as a trade-in, subtracting the profit from the price of his next vehicle.

Term

The next major element in a lease is its term: How long will you lease your vehicle? Most consumer leases today are for two- or three-year terms. Occasionally, if a customer plans to keep a vehicle a little longer, a four-year lease might be good. I recommend the two- or three-year lease because that's about the normal trade-in cycle for new-vehicle customers.

With a two- or three-year lease, the customer can walk away at the end, many times while the vehicle is still in warranty. Also, most vehicles require very little maintenance in the first three years—some oil changes and filters, and maybe one tire rotation, but that's all. Many times the marginally lower payment on the four-year lease is offset by the additional maintenance and repairs required in the fourth year.

Typically, automobile manufacturers heavily subsidize the shorter leases. In some cases, you can get a two-year lease for the same payment—or an even lower payment—you'd make on a three- or four-year lease. The manufacturers' motive, of course, is to get you into one of their new vehicles sooner so that they can sell more vehicles in any given period of time.

In the past, too many people were attracted to the five-year lease because of the very low payment. Customers who owe more on their trade-in than it is worth and don't have the cash to cover the negative equity find the five-year lease attractive because it gives them more months to amortize that negative equity (assuming that they have to add it to the lease). In effect, it keeps their payments lower. Most people, however, want a new vehicle sooner than five years. When they try to break the lease early, they find that the payoff is thousands of dollars higher than the value of the vehicle. Naturally, this leaves a very bad taste in their mouths about leasing. But the problem really lies in the customer's lack of understanding. A five-year lease gives the consumer a level payment over 60 months, but vehicles don't depreciate evenly. They depreciate much more when they are brand new. When the customer wants out of that 60-month lease—after, say, 36 or 42 months—the lease payments don't add up to anything near the actual depreciation of the vehicle. That's why the payoff is so much higher than the market value.

The situation is even worse if the customer carries negative equity into the five-year lease. In the final analysis, the consumer goes for the five-year lease to get the lowest possible payment and accommodate the negative equity in the trade. Then when she tries to break the lease early, reality sets in. The customer is better off structuring the lease in sync with her actual usage, even though her monthly payments might be higher. Customer satisfaction on five-year leases is only 9 percent. It's another case of buying the wrong shoe to save money.

GAP protection

Most, though not all, leases today include a very desirable feature known as GAP protection. Although many consumers are unaware of it, GAP protection covers the difference between any insurance settlement and the lease payoff if the vehicle is stolen or destroyed during the lease. If a vehicle is financed and stolen or totaled, the insurance company will settle for the actual cash value, which is frequently less than the amount owed on the vehicle—and the gap between the two has to be covered by the consumer. Think about that. After the accident or the theft, the consumer is still paying off a vehicle he can't even drive.

But suppose that same vehicle was leased from a company that includes GAP protection in its leases. That element of the lease means that the gap between the insurance settlement and the lease payoff is covered. The customer has a paid-up contract and can start fresh on her next vehicle. An additional benefit of GAP protection is that it covers not only the extra depreciation on the leased vehicle, but also the negative equity—if any—on the trade-in. Be sure to ask about GAP protection, because not all lease companies include it.

Getting the best deal

Mileage is an important factor in developing your lease, and it is always best to include the amount of miles you will be driving. If you will be over the standard mileage, it's usually cheaper to add the extra miles into the payment at the onset. Some people refer to this as paying the extra mileage "up front," but that's not what they're doing. They are *contracting* up front to *pay* in the monthly payments. A 20,000-mile-per-year lease would cost $33.33 a month more than a 15,000-mile-per-year lease if the additional miles were charged at 8 cents apiece. As I have already mentioned, this is far less than the actual market depreciation on a vehicle you own.

At the other end of the mileage spectrum, it is possible for the low-mileage driver to get a 10,000- or 12,000-mile-per-year lease. The residual is raised to reflect the lower mileage, and that lowers the payment. The important thing is to assess your driving realistically. Don't take a low-mileage lease just to get a lower payment, because if you exceed your allocated mileage, you will be charged about 15 cents per extra mile. Tailor the mileage to what you think your usage will be.

Some leases require a capitalized cost reduction. This lowers the monthly payment, and in some cases it may also get you a lower lease rate. On the other hand, you will not have the use of that capital. There was a time when some leasing companies *kept* the capitalized cost reductions as additional profit and didn't give customers the benefit in their payments, but that practice has been pretty much put to rest. Under the new Regulation M of the Federal Truth in Leasing Act, the capitalized cost reduction has to be shown on the face of the contract. If you want to include a capitalized cost reduction in the lease, there's nothing wrong with that, as long as you get credit for it. However, if you don't have a similar capitalized cost reduction on your next lease, the payment may jump considerably.

I explained in chapter 3 that from time to time manufacturers subsidize certain leases. It is good to find out from the dealer or independent lease company which models are subsidized. If you can't decide between two models, find out if one is more heavily subsidized than the other. That one will save you money even if it is the more expensive model, because the subsidy may lower the payment greatly.

Some leasing companies charge a disposition fee if the vehicle is returned to them at the end of the lease. This could be as much as $600. Other leasing companies do not charge a disposition fee at lease end. You should know going in what your dealer or leasing company does. Too often the customer is unaware of the disposition fee until the end of the lease. Had he known about it ahead of time, he might have chosen a different vehicle—or a different leasing company.

One final thing to consider in choosing your lease is the type of payoff calculation that will be used to determine the lease payoff if you want to get out of the lease early. Most lease companies use the Actuarial Formula, based on simple interest. This is the fairest deal for the consumer, who ends up paying only the lease charges that were incurred. However, some lease companies use the "Rule of 78s," sometimes called the "sum of the digits," to calculate the payoff when the customer wants to break the lease early. That means that more of the consumer's past payments went for lease charges and less for principal reduction, so in order to break the lease early, the consumer's payoff will be hundreds of dollars higher.

As you can see, there is a great deal more to designing your lease than just getting the lowest payment. In fact, the payment means absolutely nothing in a lease until the consumer understands all the terms and conditions of the lease. For myself, I like a 36-month, closed-end lease with a fixed option price at the end. I want 20,000 miles per year built into the lease. I want GAP protection included and no disposition fee at the end. I want the early payoff to be figured using simple interest. To get this lease, I might have to accept higher monthly payments but in the end I will be getting the best deal.

However, if you have been a cash buyer of autos, you will be interested in learning about "one-pay" or "single-pay" leases, which are described on page 59 of this book.

CHAPTER FIVE

The Biggest Problem Car Buyers Face Today

T HE TYPICAL CUSTOMER WHO GOES INTO AN automobile dealership today hoping to buy a new vehicle owes a great deal more on his trade-in than the car is worth.

Negative equity in trade-in

He is "buried in his trade" or "upside down." I estimate that this is true of somewhere between 70 and 80 percent of potential new-vehicle customers today. The average trade-in represents between $1500 and $5000 of negative equity, and this situation just keeps getting worse. That lump of negative equity can't usually be blamed only on the customer's current trade-in vehicle. Some of it was carried from the vehicle before that and the one before that and the one before that. Every time the customer trades for a new vehicle and doesn't have the cash to the cover the negative equity on the old one, he rolls that negative equity into the new loan and tops it with additional interest. In fact, the customer is making one car payment, but he's paying for four cars! At one time, the customer was surprised when the auto salesperson told him how much his negative equity was. Not so today. Customers *know* they are buried in their trades. They just ask, "How much?" The reason for this situation, as I indicated earlier, is that wages have not been increasing as rapidly as automobile prices.

Back in the 1950s, it was very common for people to trade their cars in for new vehicles every year or two. Inflation was low, and wages were in sync with the price of vehicles. Then in the 1960s inflation took hold, and the price of cars increased. Buyers began shifting to a three-year trade cycle to make new vehicles affordable. I can remember when, in the mid-1960s, banks started to offer three-year financing for the first time. As vehicles continued to increase in value, the banks went to four-year financing, five-year financing, six-year financing, and now, in some areas of the country, seven-year financing! People needed this longer-term financing to make their payments affordable if they wanted to own their vehicles. Their trading habits, however, don't include driving a car for six or seven years. They want to trade in every three to three-and-a-half years. Since the vehicle isn't worth anywhere near what the customer owes, the cash deficit is added to the next loan. Both the customer and the dealer think the longer-term financing has solved the customer's negative equity problem. In fact, it makes it worse and only defers the need to confront it.

Term is more important than payment

Years ago, car dealers sold cars. They created demand for particular vehicles. The salesperson greeted a customer, identified her needs, demonstrated a couple of vehicles, pointed out their features, and drew up a sales contract. Not any more! Today the salesperson is "a workout artist." Now, after greeting the customer, the salesperson determines the value of the trade-in, then checks out the payoff to determine the negative equity. After that, the customer picks out a new vehicle, and the salesperson goes to the new-car manager to get the lowest selling price on the new vehicle and to the used-car manager to get a "bump" on the trade appraisal. Finally, the salesperson goes to the finance manager to find out the lowest possible interest rate if they finance the vehicle for the longest possible term. If this makes the payment affordable, the customer takes the vehicle. How much selling did the salesperson do?

But even if this isn't exactly "selling," what's wrong with it? A couple of things. First, both the salesperson and the customer are very short-sighted. They aren't considering the long-term ramifications of their deal. Eighty-three percent of the people who finance their vehicles trade them in before the loan has been paid to zero. Customers who keep doing this are digging themselves into deeper and deeper holes, and salespeople who don't look beyond today's commission are part of the problem. Second, most salespeople will agree that when they lower the selling price to make the numbers work, they are using some of their profit and commission to pay off the lien holder on the trade. As the negative equity that needs to be covered gets bigger and bigger, the salesperson's commissionable gross gets smaller and smaller. If this continues, soon the potential gross isn't enough to cover the negative equity, and it becomes impossible to make a sale. This long-term financing has effectively taken the customer out of the market.

If long-term financing is not the solution to the high-priced vehicle problem, what is? Short-term leasing! The payment on a 36-month lease is about the same as on a 60-month finance contract, but after 36 months the customer has a paid-up contract. He has no negative equity to carry forward (and to pay additional interest on!).

"Selling" leasing to buyers

Unfortunately, when a salesperson suggests a short-term lease to a customer who has never leased before, the customer's reaction is usually negative. The salesperson does not pursue the issue. We know that when a customer says

he isn't interested in leasing, it's not because he understands leasing and doesn't want any part of it. It's because
he doesn't understand leasing. He has a perfectly natural
fear of the unknown. It is easier—and maybe safer—to
say "No" to something you don't understand than "Yes."
A skilled salesperson, recognizing this dynamic, will try—
without being aggressive—to educate the customer about
leasing. This salesperson should cover all the facts I went
over in chapter 3. A salesperson should take the position
not of selling leasing, but of *offering* leasing. Instead of
trying to "sell" a lease, she should think of herself as a
teacher. That means that the last thing she should do is
tell her new customer that leasing is better than buying.
That will put the customer in the position of defending
buying (which is what he came in to do and has probably
done before) against this new option he knows nothing
about. After all, he has to defend his position or acknowledge his ignorance, so he will become defensive. What do
we do when we are painted into a corner? We come out
swinging! Telling a person who has never leased that leasing is better is confrontational, even adversarial.

Instead, the salesperson can say, "Leasing is **different** from buying." That statement isn't a challenge, and it
is provable. If the salesperson takes this softer approach,
most customers will listen. Rather than tell the customer
what to do, the salesperson simply explains: "I don't know
whether leasing will benefit you or not—I really don't have
a clue. But let me explain some of the differences between

leasing and buying, and tell you about the full disclosure required under the new Federal Truth in Leasing Act. Then, you can decide for yourself whether leasing or buying is better for you." That's what I like best about being in the leasing business as long as I have. We don't use high pressure. We don't use smoke and mirrors. We don't prevaricate. We don't appeal to the customers' pseudo-psychology. All we do is state the facts and tell the truth. Once a customer understands leasing, he's likely to wonder why no one ever explained it to him before.

When a salesperson fails to fully explain leasing to a customer, she is doing the customer a disservice, because once she's been educated the customer can make an informed decision for himself. For the same reason, any customer who doesn't *let* the salesperson explain leasing is doing himself a disservice. For the customer, comparing leasing to buying is the same as comparing one model of car to another. You find out the facts, then you make up your mind. Many people have switched to leasing to solve the big problem of long-term financing and the negative equity that goes with it.

When you finance, you don't really own

Many people are not interested in leasing because they want that feeling of ownership. It is really an emotional issue for them. If they lease, they don't have any equity. True. But 95 percent of the people who buy cars finance them through the dealer, a credit union, or a bank. They *don't* own their vehicles—the lending institution owns them. And since 83 percent of financed vehicles are traded before the balance is paid to zero, the customer *never* owns "his" car. I've heard salespeople say to a customer, "You think you own the vehicle when you finance it? Just skip two payments, and you'll find out who owns it!" Or "If you think you own your vehicle when you buy it and finance it, then why do banks have drive-up windows? So cars can visit their rightful owners from time to time." In addition to considering whether you actually "own" a financed car, ask yourself "why do I *want* to own a car in the first place?" It is good to own some things— real estate, stocks and bonds, and other assets that appreciate in value. But what good does it do you to own a depreciating asset? Would you buy a house that you thought would go down in value? Would you buy stock at $100 per share if you thought it would be worth $50 per share in two years? Of course not! Then why do you want to own a vehicle? A vehicle is a depreciating asset.

When a customer responds that she wants to own the vehicle because otherwise she won't have any equity, I ask her how much equity she will have, after 36 months, in a vehicle financed for 60 months. Not only won't she have equity, she'll probably have negative equity. After 36 months on a lease, she'd have a paid-up contract.

Dealership salespeople have to work with customers who just want the lowest payment, regardless of the term of financing. The sales manager feels that to be competitive he has to offer the lowest possible payment, even if he has to stretch the financing way beyond a customer's expected usage. With a little effort, the sales manager could show the customer that term is more important than payment, because low payments over the long term can leave the customer buried in roll-over debt.

And it's worth the sales manager's effort. You don't have to offer the lowest payment to be competitive. You have to offer the most value. The increased value in a shorter-term lease more than offsets any potential higher payment. Dealership personnel should be ready and willing to explain this.

Flexibility

Consumers persist in doubting the flexibility of leasing. They argue that the customer is locked in for the term of the lease, and if he breaks the lease early he'll be hit with a big charge. That's true—as far as it goes—but in terms of getting out early, the flexibility of a lease is exactly the same as the flexibility of a loan. When you sign a loan contract, there is nothing that says you can't pay it off early. When you sign a lease contract, there is nothing that says you can't pay *it* off early. In both cases, the payoffs are figured in exactly the same way: take the initial advance and subtract whatever principal has been paid. The problem with both leases and loans is that the customer's payments are the same every month throughout the term of the contract. In effect, the contract—or lease—averages the depreciation of the vehicle. However, most people know vehicles don't depreciate on an "average" basis. They depreciate more when they are new and less as they age. Therefore, if a customer wants to get out of a lease or a loan early, the depreciation on the vehicle will amount to more than the consumer has paid. In both cases, then, the consumer will come up short. However, she won't come up as short with a short-term lease as she will with a long-term finance contract. If you own a vehicle, have a loan on it, and want to get out early, you can't just hand it back to the bank. You have to sell it. If you can't sell it for the amount you owe, you have to come up with the difference. A lease is exactly as flexible as a loan. The charge involved in breaking a lease early is *not* a penalty. It is called a **deficiency** because it is the amount necessary to make up for the vehicle's depreciation that has not yet been covered by lease payments.

Leasing and credit

Five or more years ago, you had to have perfect credit to qualify for a lease. In general, you needed better credit to lease than to buy. Today things have changed. For the most part anyone who qualifies for financing will automatically qualify for a two- or three-year lease from the captive finance companies (GMAC, Ford Credit, etc.) and independent lease companies. A number of financial institutions have learned that a lease, because of its shorter term, removes the risk of the longer-term financing. For one thing, over a longer period of time more things can go wrong, things that can affect the consumer's ability to pay off his loan.

Today many people who once would not have qualified are eligible for leases. As a matter of fact, in some cases a customer with marginal credit—normally rated a C tier and required to pay a higher interest rate on a loan—can become an A tier lease customer with a lower lease rate. There is simply less risk to the lease company because the term of the lease is shorter. The customer's lease rate is set considerably lower than her interest rate, which makes her lease payment that much lower than her loan payment would be *and the term is shorter as well!*

Leasing can solve the biggest problem many customers face today: the huge negative equity they face when they try to trade their old vehicle for a new one. The short-term payments on a lease are affordable when short-term loan financing would not be. If dealership personnel will take the time to explain leasing, they can help customers get over the emotional appeal of vehicle ownership.

CHAPTER SIX

Leasing Benefits for the Cash Buyer

O NE OF THE BIGGEST MISCONCEPTIONS ABOUT leasing is summed up in the question "If I can pay cash for a vehicle why should I lease?" That would, of course, be a valid question if leasing were just another way to purchase a vehicle—but it isn't. As more cash buyers understand the many differences between buying with cash and leasing, more of them take advantage of the benefits of leasing. Dealership personnel in general doubt that they can lease to a cash buyer, but cash buyers are just like financing buyers in one respect: they don't want to lease because they don't understand leasing, and no one has taken the time to explain it to them. In my own experience, I have actually found it easier to switch a cash buyer to a lease than a conventional finance customer to a lease.

No depreciation risk

Cash buyers tend to be very conservative, and they don't like risk. That makes leasing ideal for them because leasing removes the risk of the vehicle's depreciation. The cost of your vehicle is *not what you pay for it.* The real cost is *the vehicle's depreciation.* The used-car market—not the car owner—controls depreciation, but when you lease, depreciation is guaranteed by the leasing company. A lease is a kind of insurance policy which guarantees the future value of your asset. The more conservative you are, the less you like risk and the more you like insurance. Can you imagine trying to sell used-car futures to any customer—especially a conservative one? But that's what consumers buy when they buy a vehicle.

The best example I can give you of the advantages of leasing over cash buying happened a couple of years ago. Cadillac offered a special lease on a $40,000 Sedan Deville—a 24-month lease with no capitalized cost reduction and a very attractive payment of $498 per month. The residual Cadillac used was $27,000. That's how much they thought the car would be worth at the end of the lease. Well, the leases ended. Do you know how much those Devilles sold for? $19,000! Any consumer who took advantage of that lease got an $8000 gift from General Motors. Anyone who bought the vehicle because he just had to "own" it paid $8000 more than those who leased. Do you think customers who knew that buying was going to cost them *$8000 more* than leasing would have insisted on buying? I doubt it. That's a lot of money to pay for a "feeling" of ownership. It feels pretty good to save $8000. True, that's one instance. What if the Cadillac had been worth $30,000 at the end of the lease? Would the customer who leased regret his "mistake"? No—because he could still buy the Deville for $27,000, sell it for $30,000, and keep the $3000 profit. Leasing removes the uncertainty from depreciation.

One-payment leases

Most leasing companies today offer a lease that is ideal for a cash buyer, the "one-pay" or "single-pay" lease. It's a conventional lease with just one difference—the customer makes one payment up front, the total of the 36 monthly payments minus an interest credit because the payment is made in advance. The consumer gets all the rights and protections of a conventional lease without the bother of making monthly payments. Again, the idea is, "Why pay for the whole vehicle when you can pay only for the part used?" Instead of issuing a check for $40,000, just pay $18,000. Keep the $22,000 in the bank or in your investments. At the end of the lease, you're in a good position to decide whether or not you want to buy the vehicle. You know whether it's a good vehicle because you've been driving it. You know what your needs are now. You can have the vehicle appraised, and—if you can make a profit—

buy it. If you can't, give it back to the lease company and let it take the loss.

Wouldn't you love to see a copy of *The Wall Street Journal* three months in advance? You'd know how a given investment would work out before you committed any money to it. Well, a one-pay lease gives you the same advantage. Why commit for the whole vehicle up front when you don't have to? There is enough uncertainty in people's lives already, so why add the uncertainty of having to own a vehicle in three years, whether you want to or not? You lose nothing by leasing. It is not an either/or proposition. You never give up the right of ownership. All you do is postpone the decision. Consider the lease a three-year test drive, and decide at the end if you want to own your vehicle.

Protect your assets

Cash buyers usually have other assets, and they are more than likely to be high-income people. The limited liability offered through leasing appeals to them because they don't own the car—the leasing company does. The more income and assets a customer has, the more he appreciates the potential shelter.

If the cash buyer has investments, their yield may be much higher than the lease charges. Paying cash eliminates interest charges, and—since the rate of return on investments is usually higher than the lease rate—the net difference is a profit. Even if he doesn't have investments, the cash buyer can put the savings in the bank. Liquidity gives many people a feeling of security and peace of mind.

The cash buyer who is a high-mileage driver—that is, one who drives more that 15,000 miles per year—can also save money in a lease. Those extra miles can be purchased in the lease for less than the actual depreciation that accompanies high mileage.

GAP protection

A person who pays cash for a vehicle does not get the benefit of GAP protection. If the purchased vehicle is stolen or destroyed, the insurance company will often settle for a greatly depreciated value, so the consumer stands to lose quite a bit of money. Consumers whose leases include GAP protection won't lose a dime!

Tax benefits of leasing

Most states, as I explained in chapter 3, give consumers who lease a sales tax saving. No matter how much money people have, they don't like to pay more taxes than they have to. Purchase a vehicle and you're taxed on the full amount. Pay cash for it, and you pay that tax on the spot. With a one-pay lease, on the other hand, the sales tax is paid on the single payment, and that payment is calculated after the residual is subtracted. A lower total means a lower tax.

One final benefit leasing offers a cash buyer is a tax deduction. If the vehicle is used primarily for business purposes, the cash buyer's tax deduction is very limited. The allowable depreciation deduction is usually less than the actual depreciation, so the consumer can't even write off his real expenses. On the other hand, when the consumer leases, there is no limit to the deduction, so there could be a great tax advantage to leasing. Again, many people who might be in a position to pay cash for a vehicle don't understand leasing. When they hear it explained, they often decide that a one-pay lease would be beneficial. GMAC calls its one-pay lease The Smart/Lease Plus, and Ford Credit calls its one-pay lease the Advanced Payment Plan.

A few years ago, I visited a Cadillac dealership in Florida and asked how they were doing with leasing. The salespeople and managers all laughed and told me they didn't do any leasing at all. All their customers were elderly and very wealthy, and they paid cash for their vehicles. None of them wanted to lease. That wasn't really accurate. The fact was that those customers were never given the option to lease and never had the one-pay lease explained to them. Obviously, if you are given only one choice and don't know there are other options, you take that one choice. That's the position those Cadillac customers were in. I showed the dealership personnel how to educate their customers about leasing, how to explain the sales tax savings under Florida law, how to present leasing as an insurance policy. Sure enough, once the customers understood leasing and were given the chance to lease, many did. Today, that Cadillac dealership leases to *over 70 percent* of its customers.

Leasing is an educational process.

CHAPTER SEVEN

Why Are Dealers So Anxious to Lease?

WHY WOULD AN AUTOMOBILE DEALER WANT to lease a vehicle rather than sell it? There must be good reasons that you're seeing so many advertisements for leasing on television and in newspapers. For one thing, because leases are shorter than finance contracts, customers are in the market for new vehicles sooner and more often. What's more, customers are happier. And when customers are happy, they tend to go back to the same dealer for their next vehicle. That means increased sales for a dealership. The national average for customer retention in car sales is 25 percent. That means that, if you buy a vehicle from a particular dealer, the odds are only one in four that you will buy your next vehicle from the same dealer. The customer retention for leasing, however, is over 50 percent. If you lease, the odds more than double that you will return to the same dealer for your next vehicle. (We can presume that the happy, returning customer was put into the proper lease, one that was tailored to his needs.)

Higher customer retention

People who lease are generally happier with the transaction than those who purchase, for two important reasons: (1) Leasing is a more pleasant transaction than buying. You generally don't haggle over selling price when you're not buying anything. At the end of the lease, the customer is not responsible for the residual, so there's no need to haggle over trade-in value. Buying a vehicle can be very stressful, even downright confrontational. (2) If a lease is written for two or three years, the vehicle is under warranty for the whole period of the contract. Should something go wrong with the vehicle, the customer doesn't have to pay for repairs.

The benefits to the dealer of more satisfied customers are obvious. The customer will not only return to the dealership for her next vehicle, but be more inclined to recommend the dealership to friends and relatives. All automobile dealers are graded by their manufacturers on customer satisfaction, and the dealers with high CSIs—Customer Service Indexes—tend to get the best treatment from the manufacturers. That treatment can include anything from a bigger allocation of a hot product to the granting of additional franchises. The dealers who do the most leasing enjoy the highest CSIs.

Good used cars

Good low-mileage used vehicles are in great demand by auto dealers. If at the end of a lease, the customer does not exercise the option to buy the vehicle, the dealer has the second option. This makes good vehicles available to the dealer's used-car department. In many cases, it is a better source of used-car inventory than the auto auctions.

Dealerships whose salespeople are trained to present and explain leasing use leasing to make deals they would otherwise lose. Leasing can more flexibly meet consumers' needs because it offers a lower monthly payment, and most consumers are payment buyers. In some cases, leasing requires less up-front money so it appeals to customers who don't have much cash for a down payment. One major way that leasing can "save" a deal is by applying some of the "over advance" to cover the customer's negative equity on his trade. A lease company often pays 110 percent of the window-sticker price for a vehicle. On a $20,000 vehicle, that gives the dealer an additional $2000 to help pay off the trade-in. When a customer comes in owing more on his trade-in than it's worth and he can't come up with the difference in cash, the dealer can use the extra advance from the leasing company. This way, the customer gets the new vehicle he wants, and the dealer gets another sale. It is not additional profit for the dealer. Everyone wins.

Increasing sales and service

Overall, leasing increases a dealer's sales by making the product more affordable and by bringing customers back to do more business. Automobile dealers who do the most leasing can counteract the cyclical nature of the auto business. They can make their dealerships recession-proof.

One big problem faced by dealers today is personnel turnover. The cyclical nature of the business makes it hard to keep good salespeople. A dealer who is very active in leasing, however, tends to have less turnover because of the high customer retention. That benefits both the dealer and the salesperson. A salesperson who has built-in, returning business has less incentive to leave the dealer.

Service and parts departments and collision repair shops are also important profit centers for a dealer. Customers who lease tend to take their vehicles back to the selling dealer for this work.

Leasing and dealer profits

Many people are concerned that dealers push leasing just to increase their profits, that leasing takes the customer's attention off the selling price and the dealer can make more money. That may or may not be the case. In general, leasing is no different from selling for profit. Several factors apply in both cases.

1. Supply and demand usually set the amount of profit for the dealer in either a lease or a sale.
2. How badly the dealer wants to get rid of a vehicle is also important.
3. The customer's ability to negotiate a good deal will affect the outcome.

In a lease, part of the gross profit is often used to pay the negative equity on the customer's trade-in. In many cases, the profit on a lease is less than on a sale. Most manufacturers offer lease specials from time to time, and in those instances they subsidize the lease rate and the residual. To make the leases even more attractive for the consumer, manufacturers then limit the amount of the gross profit the dealer can make. In those situations, the dealer *definitely* makes less on a lease than on a sale. In some cases, the customer likes all the benefits of leasing, it fits her budget, and she isn't concerned about negotiating a lower capitalized cost. Then the dealer might make more on a lease than on a sale. There are also situations in which the manufacturer's incentives built into the lease are greater than the increase in the dealer's profit. Then the dealer makes a bigger profit, and the customer saves money as well because that increased dealer profit comes from the manufacturer, not from the customer. If you decide to lease a vehicle that is advertised for sale at a particular price, be certain that the same price is used as the capitalized cost.

At one time, dealers regularly offered a given vehicle for sale at a certain price, then switched the customer to a lease and raised the selling price to the leasing company. This automatically raised the dealer's profit—and the customer had no idea what was happening. The use of non-disclosed leases (the capitalized cost of the vehicles was not shown on the contract) made this practice possible. These leases have been illegal since January 1, 1998, when the new Federal Truth in Leasing Act was put in place. Under Regulation M, it mandates disclosure in the lease of many facts, one of which is the capitalized cost. Now the consumer can see what costs make up the lease payment, how much the leasing company paid for the vehicle, plus any other charges, such as a service agreement or credit insurance. No dealer can automatically increase his gross profit by switching a customer to a lease.

You can see that there are many reasons why a dealer would rather lease than sell a vehicle. Most of those reasons boil down to the shorter trade cycle, which makes customers happier and smoothes out the peaks and valleys of the dealer's business cycle.

CHAPTER EIGHT

The Biggest Abuses in Leasing

VEHICLE LEASING, LIKE EVERY OTHER COMMER-
cial transaction, can be good or bad. Selling
drugs is good if you're a pharmacist providing
antibiotics; selling drugs is bad if you're a "dealer" ped-
dling at a schoolyard.

There are reasons that the transaction of leasing got
a bad reputation. In the past, a lot of abuses went unre-
ported and even unacknowledged. For instance, it was
fairly common for a salesperson to grab a quick commission by putting a customer into a lease that was not at all
in the best interest of the customer. The salesperson could
get by with this because there are so many types of leases
and so few people who really understand leasing. Under
such conditions, it was absurdly easy to steer the consumer
to the lowest-payment lease, even though it probably wasn't
tailored to meet his needs.

Don't get burned

A lease that *is* tailored to the consumer's needs will probably be a better deal than buying the vehicle would be. But getting into the *wrong* lease can turn out to be a nightmare for the customer, so if you decide to lease a vehicle, be very careful and be sure you understand what you are doing. This chapter will help you play it safe.

In chapter 4, I told you about the abuses arising from putting a customer into an open-end rather than a closed-end lease. Offering an open-end lease wasn't *necessarily* an abuse, but such leases are tailored to business or commercial leasing because they require the *customer* to guarantee the lease-end residual. Uninformed customers, attracted by artificially low monthly payments, were duped into guaranteeing unrealistically high residuals. At the end of the lease, when the vehicle was sold for less than the guaranteed residual, the customer had to make up the difference—which usually came as a complete surprise. When the lease was originally drawn up, the salesperson more often than not told the customer, "Don't worry about guaranteeing the residual. The vehicle will be worth that much at the end." The customer didn't know any better, so he signed the lease and then got hit with a large bill-back at the end. Unfortunately, many customers couldn't pay the bill-back, so the whole transaction left negative marks on their credit reports.

With better informed consumers and new leasing legislation, open-end leases are rarely offered to today's consumers. (In fact, in some states they are illegal.) Even if a consumer *does* enter into an open-end lease, the maximum bill-back, under federal law, is the equivalent of three monthly payments. Suppose you are in an open-end consumer lease guaranteeing a $12,000 residual. At the end of the lease, the vehicle is worth only $10,000, so your deficiency is $2000. However, since your payments are $300 per month, federal law says that the leasing company can bill you back only $900—the equivalent of three months' payments! Nevertheless, I don't recommend open-end leases for consumers.

What to look for in a lease

Customers must also pay attention to the option to purchase at the end of the lease. Most lease companies give a fixed option, which means that at the inception of the lease the customer already knows how much the vehicle will cost if she wants to buy it at the end of the lease. It does not say she *has to* buy it, only that she can if she chooses to. Even if you don't think you will be interested in buying the vehicle at the end, you should still insist on a fixed option. If the vehicle is worth more than your option at the end of the lease but you don't want to keep it, you can buy it, sell it, and keep the profit. In recent years many models—especially trucks and sport utility vehicles—have been worth more than the fixed option. That means a profit for the customer. Without the fixed option, that profit goes to the lease company. Why should the company get that windfall profit?

Some lease companies offer no option to purchase; others offer only a "fair market option." As I asked in chapter 4: "What market—wholesale or retail? And who decides what's 'fair'?" Stick with the fixed option lease, because you never know what your vehicle might be worth at the end.

Avoid the pitfall of signing a long-term lease just to get a very low payment. It's true that the longer the lease, the lower the payment, but *term is more important than payment.* Why? If you sign a lease for 60 or 66 months and want to get out early, you may have to come up with thousands of dollars because the value of the vehicle is generally far less than the lease payoff. To satisfy your contract, you must either pay the difference in cash or add it to your next vehicle contract. Both choices are very painful, and you're stuck with them because your payments on the longer-term lease were so low that too little money was applied to principal reduction on your contract. Meanwhile, your vehicle has depreciated more than you have paid toward the principal, and you're facing a huge deficit. You can avoid this problem with a shorter-term lease. Your monthly payment will be higher, but you will have a paid-up contract after two or three years. It clearly makes better business sense to pay for something while you are using it than to be hit with a major expense at the end of your use.

The standard consumer lease offers 15,000 free miles per year and charges approximately 8 to 15 cents per mile for additional miles. Low-mileage leases—offering 10,000 to 12,000 miles per year—are also available. The advantage of these leases is that the residual is raised about two percentage points to reflect the lower mileage. On a $20,000 vehicle, that is $400, which lowers your payment about $11 per month on a 36-month lease. If you're really a low-mileage driver, this lease is great, but don't take it just to get that lower payment if you're likely to exceed that mileage. The vehicle-usage charge for the additional miles over your allocation will be at least 15 cents a mile and can go all the way up to 50 cents a mile. Before you sign the lease, be sure all the miles you expect to drive are included in the contract.

The Federal Truth in Leasing Act

A major—but not at all common—abuse of leasing was documented on national television in 1996. Consumers trading in their old vehicles for new, leased vehicles were not being given the fair wholesale market value for their used cars. In the worst cases, the customers got *nothing at all* for their trade-ins. The dealer just "swallowed them" as additional profit. The attorneys-general of several states got wind of this practice and cracked down. I don't understand this behavior. There are enough advantages in leasing to benefit everyone. The dealer doesn't need to steal a customer's trade-in. But to avoid being taken advantage of, find out exactly how much you are getting for your trade-in. Look at the trade-in and the new lease as separate transactions. Don't combine the two, because that just muddies the waters. Since January 1, 1998, when the new Federal Truth in Leasing Act took effect, all consumer leases in all states have to show the trade-in's equity as a capitalized cost reduction on the lease contract. That makes it relatively easy to prevent the dealer from swallowing your used car.

Read your lease carefully to be sure that any money put toward the lease—other than license, title, tax, and acquisition fees—is used as a cap cost reduction and reflected in a lower monthly payment. If these monies are not applied to the capitalized cost of the vehicle, they will not lower your monthly payment. Instead, they will simply be additional profit for the dealer. Like trade-in equity, all capitalized cost reductions must be indicated on the lease contract under the Federal Truth in Leasing Act.

There is another practice that—although it is perfectly legal—you want to be aware of and avoid. Sometimes a dealer will raise the selling price of a vehicle when you switch from buying to leasing. Here's how it works: The dealer offers a vehicle for sale at a very discounted and attractive price. An interested customer is then informed about leasing and finds the lower lease payments attractive. During the negotiations, the selling price to the lease company is raised, giving the dealer additional profit.

As I said, this practice is not illegal. It's not even techni-cally unethical, because the customer isn't *buying* the car. But it is a situation the consumer wants to avoid. Under the new Federal Truth in Leasing Act, the capitalized cost is spelled out on the contract, and that includes the sell-ing price to the leasing company. It's easy to see whether the sale price is close to the capitalized cost used by the leasing company. The facts are spelled out in the contract, and consumers can act accordingly.

The Federal Truth in Leasing Act does address the consequences for the consumer of breaking the lease early. It is really impossible to know, at lease signing, how much of a deficiency the customer will be charged for this, because the deficiency will be the difference between the lease payoff and the market value of the vehicle. The lease payoff should be easy to determine, but the market value is the big unknown. Many factors come into play: the age, model, miles, and condition of the vehicle; the season of the year; and the general market conditions. All these have a bearing on the market value of the leased vehicle, and they are impossible to forecast with any certainty. You can't expect to be told at the outset exactly what it will cost to prematurely terminate your lease, but you can avoid any premature deficiency by leasing for only as long as you intend to keep the vehicle.

What if your circumstances change? What if some-thing happens that causes you to want to terminate your lease early? You can't be told just how much that will cost, but you can insist that the lease include a formula for determining what the payoff will be to break the contract early. Otherwise, you are at the mercy of the dealer or lease company if you try to break the contract early. In some cases, the consumer can't even get a payoff from the lease company, only from the original dealer—and if he doesn't get his next vehicle from that same dealer, his payoff goes up! That is an abuse of leasing. The customer is locked in. In my opinion, that arrangement takes unfair advantage of the consumer. Ideally, when you sign a lease, you should be given a formula *or* a printout similar to a home mortgage specifying what the payoff will be at any given time during the lease. This doesn't tell you what it will cost to break the lease, but it does specify the payoff, and it doesn't leave you at anyone's mercy.

Finally, I want to make you aware of a kind of misrepresentation you might come upon if you decide to lease. No matter what newspaper I read or television advertisement I see, all the manufacturers and dealers are offering leases, most of them with very, very low payments. A $24,000 vehicle might be offered on a three-year lease for a monthly payment of only $169. Very attractive. That monthly payment appears in very big print, but the fine print informs you that, to be eligible for the very low payment, you must come up with between $1000 and $5000 as a capitalized cost reduction. People are lured into the dealership by the low payment, not realizing how much money is required up front. A lot of consumers don't have that kind of cash on hand. As I said, such advertising is not illegal, but you should watch out for it. The rule in any consumer transaction is, "If it looks too good to be true, it probably is." Leasing offers many benefits you can't get when you buy, but it is not a free ride.

I set out in this chapter to explain some of the worst and most common abuses in leasing. Since the Federal Truth in Leasing Act took effect on January 1, 1998, all consumer leasing must be done on full-disclosure leases. The information necessary to avoid being taken advantage of is shown on the contract, so the consumer now has the facts to make an intelligent decision about leasing. I am pleased with the new law because it removes a lot of suspicion and skepticism about leasing, it will eliminate the most common abuses, and it allows educated consumers to protect themselves.

How to judge whether you're getting a good deal

I've said this before, but it bears repeating: consumers make a big mistake if they simply look for the lowest lease payment. Leasing is different from buying, because instead of pricing a vehicle, you are pricing the lease. You can always get a lower lease payment by altering the terms and conditions of the lease. The important thing is to get a lease that suits your needs. Remember—the lease payment means absolutely nothing unless all the terms and conditions of the lease are right for you.

Here is my advice:

1. Deal only with well-established businesses. You can check their reputations with the Better Business Bureau or your consumer protection agencies. Friends and relatives are also good sources of information about the reputation of a business.

2. Tailor the lease to your own situation and needs. I recommend a closed-end lease with a fixed option to buy at the end.

3. The term of the lease should be the period of time you really intend to keep the vehicle.

4. Be sure your expected mileage is built into the lease and included in the payment.

5. Ask for GAP protection.

6. Make sure the trade equity or cap-cost reduction is stated on the contract and is reflected in the payment.

7. Find out how the payoff will be calculated should you decide to terminate the lease early.

8. Don't focus entirely on any one thing—the trade-in value of your old vehicle, the capitalized cost of the new vehicle, or the payment. Look at the whole picture—what you are getting in the lease, the value you place on what you are getting, the total amount you are paying.

The best way to judge whether you are getting a good deal, after you understand the terms and conditions of the lease, is to look at the sum total of the payments (which is spelled out in the lease). That tells you what you are paying for what you are getting. With that figure, you can judge the lease's value to you. Remember chapter 3? Choosing a lease just because it offers the lowest payment is like buying shoes that don't fit just because they're the cheapest shoes in the store. It will turn out to be a very painful experience.

CHAPTER NINE

Commercial Leasing

WHILE CONSUMER LEASING'S TREMENDOUS growth has taken place primarily in the last ten years, business users of vehicles have found value in leasing since the 1930s. Some, but not all, of the benefits of leasing are shared by both consumers and commercial lessees. This chapter deals with small businesses, professionals who use their vehicles for business, and large national fleets.

The vast majority of consumer leasing today is done through automobile dealers. This is a natural for dealers, because they have the franchise, the facility, and the inventory. The typical individual or family acquires one vehicle at a time, usually from an automobile dealer. Many auto dealers are equipped to offer consumer leasing as well, and those that aren't will be in the future, or they will suffer a sizable loss of market share.

Independent lease companies

Business leasing, on the other hand, is done primarily by independent lease companies which may have common ownership with a car dealer, but which operate separately and in a location removed from the dealership. An independent lease company, in many cases, is better able to service a business fleet because it is equipped to lease all makes and models, not just the one or two brands that most dealers handle. Some of the businesses that lease vehicles have been in business for twenty to thirty years, and they tend to stay with the same leasing company because they've developed a relationship of trust, much as they have with their attorneys or accountants.

Leasing frees up time and money

For businesses, the biggest advantage of leasing is that leasing frees up both time and money, which can be better invested in the business itself. Most businesses succeed because of experience, connections, and knowledge of their products or services. It makes sense for business people to devote their time to what they do best—manage their business—and to let a lease company do what it does best—manage its fleet of vehicles.

The cost of money for lease companies is very close to the prime rate. The average rate of return for small businesses has historically been twice that. The leasing company's cost of funds is about half the rate of return the business would yield if it invested its funds in its own business. So businesses are better off using the assets of a lease company and keeping their own funds at work in their own businesses. This is sometimes referred to as leverage.

Easier budgeting and off-balance-sheet financing

Many businesses rely on bank borrowing and lines of credit for ongoing cash needs and growth. Because leasing is not considered a liability, it enables a business to give its bankers a healthier financial statement and thus to be viewed more favorably. In an audited statement lease obligations are listed as "notes to the financial statement"—an obligation of the business. For borrowing purposes, however, they are not considered liabilities according to generally accepted accounting practices. This is why accountants refer to leasing as "off-balance-sheet financing."

Most businesses operate on a one-, two-, or five-year budget or plan. Vehicles are a fairly big capital expenditure, and there is a great deal of uncertainty as to their ultimate expense and depreciation. Just as for the consumer, the cost of vehicles for a business is not what the business pays for them, but the *difference* between what the business pays and what the vehicles will sell for at the end of usage. Only in a closed-end lease is the business assured of the vehicles' actual cost. It removes the risk from depreciation, so the business is better able to budget and plan.

A very common misconception about business leasing is that it is more expensive than purchasing the vehicles direct from a dealer. The lease company, in this view, is a middleman who adds overhead and profit. Won't the business save money by eliminating the middleman? Not necessarily! Here are the economics of an independent lease company: A lease company buys hundreds, if not thousands, of vehicles a year, so it gets a lower price from the dealer than the average business would. In addition, lease companies often get fleet rebates from the manufacturers, rebates that are not available to other customers, and they pass these savings on to their lessees. Usually a lease company's cost of funds is less than its client's rate of return on investments. Furthermore, a lease company can recondition the off-lease vehicle and sell it for more than the average business could. Finally, through accelerated depreciation, the lease company gets income tax advantages that are not available to other businesses. The bottom line is that a lease company can own a vehicle over a period of time for less cost than the average business can. The lease company keeps half of this cost saving to cover its overhead and as profit. It passes the other half on to the client. The net result for the business or professional person is that she gets all the benefits of leasing with a smaller total cash outlay.

The economics of the leasing business is the same as the economics of the travel business. If you are going to take a trip, there are two ways to buy your ticket: You can go to the airport two hours before flight time, stand in line, and wait for a ticket agent to write your ticket. Or you can call a travel agent over the phone, give him your credit card number, and have your ticket sent to you. That way, you can go to the airport 30 minutes before your flight and save all the hassle. In both cases, the ticket price is the same. So how does the travel agent make money if he sells tickets for the same price as the airlines? It's simple. He gets an 8 percent rebate from the airlines. The agent's profit comes not from the customer but from the airlines. The leasing business works the same way. The leasing companies don't make their money from their customers—they make it from their purchasing and borrowing power from the manufacturers' rebates, and income tax incentives.

The 1986 Tax Reform Act

For many years it's been supposed that leasing isn't beneficial for you unless you use the vehicles for business. Today there is a potential tax benefit for the business user of a vehicle, but that is an *additional* benefit. It isn't as though leasing wouldn't make sense without the tax savings. Prior to 1984, leasing companies and other businesses all had the same investment tax credits and accelerated depreciation available to them for purchasing cars. Then the Luxury Car Bill provision became law. This limited the tax savings for businesses other than vehicle-leasing companies. For the first time, commercial leasing offered a tax benefit. The leasing company could share this tax saving with their clients through lower payments. Then in 1986 the Tax Reform Act was passed, eliminating the investment tax credit for all businesses. However, the Luxury Car provision still exempted businesses that leased rather than purchased their cars. Although the tax tables have risen over the years with the consumer price index, that law is still in place.

The law says that anyone who buys a car and uses it for business can take only a very limited amount of depreciation as a tax deduction. The limited depreciation is the same regardless of the price of the vehicle, so a car owner's write-off does not increase with the price of the car. But if the businessperson leases her car and documents proper business usage, the write-off is the percentage of business usage times the lease payment—and there is no limit! If the lease payment is higher for a more expensive car on a shorter lease, the write-off will be higher. When a vehicle is leased by an employer to be driven by an employee, the driver's personal use of the vehicle must be accounted for. If the vehicle's value is over $15,500, a small income inclusion amount must be taken into account. This chapter does not attempt to offer accounting advice to the reader. For specific examples, consult your own tax advisor. The most current information printed by the Department of the Treasury can be found in Publication 463, published in December 1996.

In many cases, depending on the price of the vehicle, the mileage driven, and the percentage of business usage, leasing may turn out to be better for a business than owning that same vehicle. In any event, don't view leasing as beneficial only if there is a more generous tax treatment. You want to take all the facts into consideration in making your final decision.

CHAPTER TEN

Used-Car Leasing

ECENT STATISTICS SHOW THAT IN THE LAST FEW years the used-car leasing business has grown faster than new-vehicle leasing—not in gross volume, but as a percentage of used-car sales. This growth in used-vehicle leasing has occurred for the same reason as the growth in new-vehicle leasing— the high cost of used cars. Historically, every time the average price of new vehicles increases $100, the average price of used vehicles goes up $50. The average price of a used vehicle today is $12,000, and that price increase exceeds increases in peoples' earnings. More people, then, are turning to leasing in order to afford a good, late-model, used vehicle. Since a residual is used to calculate monthly lease payments, a lease payment will be 30 to 40 percent lower than a buy payment over the same term.

Terms and payments

Which used vehicles qualify for leasing? Well, that depends on the lease company you are using. The general rule is that lease cars will range from current-year models to three-year-old vehicles. That means that in 1998 you could lease a 1998, 1997, 1996, or 1995 model. The mileage restrictions also vary by lease company. The usual standard mileage allowance is 15,000 miles per year of life, and upward or downward adjustments are made based on the actual mileage of the vehicle to be leased. These adjustments are added to or subtracted from the residual to determine the monthly payment. For example, if a vehicle has 10,000 more miles on it than the standard allowance, the residual will be adjusted at, typically, 8 cents per mile. Eight cents times 10,000 miles is $800, so $800 is subtracted from the standard residual. The lower residual means a higher monthly payment. You calculate the effective payment increase by dividing $800 by the number of months in the lease. If the vehicle's mileage is *less* than the standard allowance, the reverse happens. A mileage credit is *added* to the residual and the payment is lowered!

Most used-vehicle leases are for a period of three years. Two- and four-year leases are being written, but they are not that attractive for the consumer. The two-year lease often makes the payment too high for the consumer; and the four-year lease doesn't offer enough savings, compared with a three-year lease, to offset the disadvantage of the longer term.

Most people who buy late-model used vehicles finance them for 60 months. Compare a 60-month finance payment with a 36-month lease payment. Which will be lower depends on both the vehicle and the residual. With new vehicles—because of manufacturers' subsidies—the lease payment will often be lower than the buy payment, even though the term is shorter. There are no manufacturers' subsidies in used-vehicle leasing, however, so the lease rates are higher and the residuals are lower. That's why the lease payment on a used vehicle might well be higher than the buy payment, if you are not comparing similar lease and loan terms.

The big attraction in used-vehicle leasing is the shorter-term contract, the shorter obligation. This offers two big benefits. First, after 36 months the consumer has a paid-up contract and no negative equity to be rolled into the next contract. Second, the customer is driving a newer vehicle requiring less maintenance and fewer repairs. To compare the difference in *actual cash outlay* between buying and leasing, you need to add the additional expense of the extra repairs on a vehicle financed for 60 months to the total of the finance payments. When you do that, the numbers heavily favor leasing. You have to look at the whole picture—including term and upkeep costs—not just at the payments.

Why lease a used vehicle?

Used-vehicle leasing offers many of the same benefits as new-vehicle leasing:

1. In many states, the customer gets a sales tax saving.
2. Lease companies may offer GAP protection.
3. Used-vehicle leases give the customer the same high-mileage savings as new-vehicle leases.
4. If the used vehicle is used for business, leasing offers a better income tax deduction.
5. One of the biggest benefits of used-car leasing (as of new-car leasing) is that the customer carries no risk of depreciation. He knows exactly what his transportation costs will be, and he is not at the mercy of the risky and uncertain used-car market.

If you lease a used vehicle, I recommend that you insist on the inclusion of a mechanical service agreement. It will add a few dollars a month to the payment, but you will have the security of knowing that, if major repairs are required, they won't come out of your pocket.

Leasing or buying a used vehicle

Sometimes people ask me, "How does used-car leasing compare with new-car leasing?" When the question is put in those terms, I have to answer, "Not that well"—because new-car leases are typically subsidized by the manufacturers, and used-car leases are not. That means that a 36-month lease payment on a current-model vehicle will often be about the same as a 36-month lease payment on a one- or two-year-old vehicle. In addition, the new vehicle comes with a full warranty. Clearly, most people would find the new-vehicle lease more attractive. On the other hand, if you were planning to purchase the vehicle at the end of the lease, the total outlay—payments and residual—on the used vehicle would be quite a bit less than that on the new one. If you were planning on returning the vehicle to the lease company at the end of the lease, that would not matter.

The real question for many people, however, is not whether to lease a new vehicle or a used one. They have already decided they would rather have a used vehicle so their neighbors won't think they're suckers for paying the manufacturers' high prices. Having definitely decided on a used vehicle, they have to decide whether to buy it or lease it.

Some car dealers don't even offer used-car leasing because they don't think it's a good deal for the customer. After all, a customer can lease a new vehicle for about the same payment as a used vehicle. But, then they will sell the used vehicle to the customer! If leasing the used vehicle isn't such a good idea, would buying it be any better? Dealers have to understand that not everyone *wants* to drive a new vehicle. If the customer has decided to drive a used vehicle home, the issue is simply how she is going to pay for it. Too many dealers make the mistake of doing their customers' thinking for them.

The dealers who do the most used-car leasing are the ones with trained salespeople who can present leasing to every qualified customer on every qualified used vehicle without prejudice—that is, without determining whether a customer would, could, or should lease. These salespeople just explain leasing and let the customers think for themselves.

Independent used-car dealers tend to do better with used-car leasing than new-car dealers because they are not tempted to try to talk a used-car customer into a new vehicle. After all, they don't sell new vehicles. Once the customer has picked out the vehicle he wants, the dealer explains how leasing works, and the customer often chooses leasing over buying—the main benefit being, as I've indicated, the shorter-term contract.

CHAPTER ELEVEN

Who Should Lease— and Who Shouldn't?

MANY PEOPLE SHOPPING FOR CARS TODAY KNOW very little about vehicle leasing—and what little they do know is either wrong or confused. A number of them don't know the difference between leasing and renting. As a result, if a salesperson tries to discuss leasing, the customer says she isn't interested. Naturally, the salesperson doesn't want to blow a potential sale by irritating the customer, so he usually drops the subject and sells the customer a vehicle. The customer never finds out how she could have benefited by leasing.

When a customer says he isn't interested in leasing, he usually doesn't know much about it, and he's reluctant to deal with an unknown transaction. It is easier to say no to something you don't understand than to learn more about it and say yes. Maybe the customer is embarrassed to admit this lack of knowledge to a salesperson. In any case, more and more people are leasing because they have taken the time to learn about it. Once they understand it, they prefer leasing to buying.

I hope the previous chapters have explained how leasing works and what to look for if you are considering leasing a vehicle. I have explained the many benefits and pointed out some of the pitfalls of leasing. No commercial transaction—including leasing—is perfect, and you can certainly run into problems with a lease. Nevertheless, if you compare leasing with buying, you'll see that any problems that can occur when you lease a vehicle can also arise when you finance one. You give up nothing by leasing, but you give up all the rights, protections, and assurances of leasing when you buy.

Who *shouldn't* lease?

Who is *not* a good candidate for leasing? Definitely anyone in the armed services who expects to be shipped overseas and wants to take a vehicle along. If you are looking for a new vehicle and plan to be relocated overseas in the next six to twelve months, leasing is not for you. You have to show proof of ownership in order to ship a vehicle overseas, and you don't have ownership when you lease. That means you'd have to terminate the lease early, buy the vehicle, and probably finance it. It would be a bigger hassle than it's worth.

Leasing is also not for anyone with a poor driving record. The costs of the mandatory public liability insurance would be likely to outweigh the benefits and savings of leasing. Lease companies usually require minimum liability coverage of $100,000/$300,000/$50,000 because they own the vehicle. As the owner, the company is primarily responsible for any damage the vehicle does. The driver may or may not be sued, but in most cases, the lease company *will* be sued. The lease company is named as "additional named insured" on the insurance policy, with the minimum limits, so it very wisely will not lease to anyone who cannot carry the required amount of coverage. A person with a poor driving record might not qualify for those limits, and even if she did qualify, the premiums would be sky high!

Anyone who carries less than the required insurance and still feels that the increased premium outweighs the benefits of leasing should not lease. However, I would argue that everyone who can should carry the higher limits. Don't view the increased premium as a penalty for leasing. Instead, consider that the increased premium is going toward increased insurance coverage and increased value in leasing. Maybe adding the lease payment to the increased premium means the consumer doesn't save any money, but at least he can now afford the amount of insurance he should have been carrying in the first place. Most people are not aware that the more liability insurance they buy, the cheaper it is per thousand dollars. The *premiums* do go up with increased coverage, but the *rates* actually go down. Anyone whose driving record precludes him from carrying the necessary insurance coverage is also precluded from the many benefits of leasing.

Anyone with unlimited cash and no particular economic use for it might not benefit from leasing either. Granted, such people are rare, but they do exist. They can't relate to the idea that they could make better use of their money than tying it up in a vehicle because they have so much money that any further increase in income is not important to them. I still think the sales tax savings and limited liability should matter to them, but in some cases even those factors are unimportant. It's just easier for them to write a check for the whole vehicle and have it over with. Such people don't care about depreciation because when they are finished with a car, they simply give it away. This is a very small category, but for the person who fits into it, leasing may not be beneficial.

If a consumer understands leasing and finds no advantage in it, so be it. I never try to dictate anyone else's priorities, so I don't argue with the customer who has an emotional attachment to ownership. If he understands leasing and admits that leasing might be better for him, but he still prefers to purchase, I know that he is being emotional rather than rational. If not owning his vehicle would cause him emotional distress and perhaps keep him awake at night, leasing is not for him.

Who *should* lease?

Anyone who operates on a budget and likes to save money would benefit by looking into leasing.

The first type of consumer who clearly benefits is the one who trades her vehicle every two, three, or four years. Leasing makes a shorter trade cycle affordable. At the end of the lease, the consumer has a paid-up contract with no negative equity to carry over to the next vehicle. She has avoided huge repair bills and saved money on maintenance because the vehicle is under warranty.

The consumer who wants to lay out less cash on a monthly basis and doesn't want to bear the risk of depreciation also benefits through leasing. With a closed-end lease, any loss is absorbed by the lease company and any profit goes to the consumer. What other transaction gives you the chance of profit without the risk of loss?

Anyone who drives more than 15,000 miles per year will definitely save through leasing. The extra miles cost a lessee about half what they cost a car owner. It surprises me that some people don't realize the effect of mileage on the value of their trade-ins. The more miles a consumer drives, the more money leasing saves him.

In most states there is a sales tax saving in leasing, though many people don't realize it. It is almost the American way not to overpay taxes, and businesses and professional people may well find an income tax benefit in leasing.

Cash buyers can benefit from a single-payment lease. They get all the rights and protection of leasing along with the upside profit potential of ownership. At the same time, they eliminate the two biggest disadvantages of ownership—risk of depreciation and liability. And they don't even make monthly payments! Once cash buyers understand the single-payment lease, they wonder why anyone would ever again pay cash for a vehicle.

People who plan to keep a vehicle for an extended period of time still benefit from leasing because in most leases they don't give up the right of ownership. They simply postpone the day they have to make the decision. If things change and after three years they want to get rid of the leased vehicle, they just give it back. They might not be able to sell a purchased vehicle for the amount they could have saved by leasing. They might not be able to sell it at all. Leasing offers customers a major benefit—the right to change their minds.

Customers looking for the best deal from the manufacturers often find it in leasing because so many models are offered on subsidized leases. Either the lease rates are lower than market rates, or the residuals are higher than market value, or both. This means a lower cash outlay than buying.

Finally, consumers with marginal credit benefit from leasing. Anyone rated at the low end of the scale—say, a C or D customer—would be charged the very highest interest rate on a car loan. By switching to a lease he automatically becomes an A tier customer for some models, which dramatically lowers his rate. This is a real cash saving for the consumer.

Is leasing right for you?

These are examples of people who would benefit from leasing and people who would not. It is up to you, the consumer, to figure out which category you fall into. The important thing is to understand leasing. Deal with a reputable dealer or independent lease company, someone who can fully explain to you the benefits of both ownership and leasing. Stay away from any dealer or salesperson who flatly states that leasing is no good. That immediately tells you that you are not talking to a trained professional. You are talking to someone who is telling you to buy only because *he* doesn't understand leasing. He can't explain it to you, and he doesn't want to look foolish. You, as the consumer, are entitled to all the information about both leasing and buying so that you can decide for yourself which would be better. Don't give up control of the decision making. Knowledge is power!

CHAPTER TWELVE

The Final Decision

I WROTE THIS BOOK TO EDUCATE CONSUMERS ABOUT leasing and help them make informed decisions. Instead of just trying to talk people into leasing, I wanted to point out the positives and the negatives. I believe that the better informed the consumer is, the better it is for all parties. In my view, if a consumer gets into a bad lease, it isn't just the fault of the salesperson. The consumer is also at fault because he looked for the wrong things in a lease.

Look at leasing with an open mind. Don't think that just because you have never leased, it must be bad. Don't be afraid of the unknown. Without people who were willing to try something new, we wouldn't have electricity, television, microwaves, or personal computers.

It is easy to show that consumer leasing has grown dramatically over the past several years, and there must be reasons for this growth. Surely not all of these people were simply fooled. So let go of any prejudices you might have against leasing. Many "facts" about it —including information put forth by some consumer reporters—are just plain incorrect. Even some consumer reporters get leasing and renting mixed up, which leads to a great deal of confusion.

After you have decided on a particular model, try to find out all you can about leasing that model. Don't be afraid to ask questions. Find out if the lease is subsidized. Be leery of the salesperson who is merely pushing the lowest payment. She is probably taking the path of least resistance. Be sure your lease suits your driving needs in regard to both term and mileage. Be sure it also meets your financial needs in regard to up-front money, mileage, Gap protection, and fixed option to purchase at the end. Now that full-disclosure leasing is mandated by federal law, it is easier to evaluate a lease in terms of capitalized cost, lease charges, and total cash outlay.

After you have designed a lease that suits you, compare it with the financial arrangement you could make when buying the same vehicle. Ask yourself these questions:

- Is the lower capital outlay in leasing beneficial to me?
- Do I have other uses for my funds than investing them in a depreciating asset?
- Do I want to trade every two or three years?

- Would I like to avoid huge repair bills?
- Is avoiding the risk of depreciation important to me?
- Do I want to save on taxes?
- Do I find value in Gap protection?
- Do these benefits outweigh the emotional feelings of ownership?
- Is fear of the unknown keeping me from trying something new?
- Am I gun-shy because of old open-end lease horror stories?
- Has information gathered from the Internet only made me more confused?

Take all these things into consideration. I believe that if you take the time to educate yourself about leasing, develop a lease that meets your needs, and deal with a reputable company, you will more than likely find leasing better than buying. My first-time lease customers usually have one of three reactions—"Oh, I didn't know it was this easy." "Oh, I thought only huge corporations qualified for leasing." And the most common reaction, "This sounds too good to be true. What's the catch? What's the gimmick?" There is no catch. There is no gimmick. It's just that no one has taken the time to explain what leasing is all about.

Under the new Federal Truth in Leasing Act, if you do feel you were taken advantage of because the leasing company didn't disclose some pertinent information, you have legal recourse. Don't hesitate to use it. The new law was enacted to correct any unscrupulous practices in leasing. Eventually, it will weed out the bad apples, and that will be better not only for the consumer, but for the leasing industry as a whole.

The best part about leasing is that we don't have to pretend that it's something it isn't. All we need to do is state the facts. Leasing is an educational process. If you decide to try leasing, become as knowledgeable as possible. Tailor the lease specifically to your needs. Don't make the common mistake of going for the lowest payment. Review all the disclosed information in the lease to be sure you are getting the very best deal. If you do all this, chances are you will find leasing to be both a good business decision and a very pleasant experience.

J. D. Power and Associates, the Agoura Hills, California, market research firm, conducted a study in 1995. The results indicated that 93 percent of lessees lease their next vehicles. That means the odds are better than eighteen to one that if you try leasing, you will like it enough to do it again when you get your next vehicle. If for some reason you find that you are uncomfortable with leasing, you can always go back to owning. What have you got to lose?

The most important things to remember are:

1. Become as educated about leasing as possible.
2. Price the lease, not the vehicle.

When you lease—and, for that matter, in every commercial transaction—it's not only what you *pay* that matters. It's what you *get* for what you pay. Leasing is all about value.

The final decision is YOURS!

Motor Vehicle Lease Agreement—Page 1

Motor Vehicle Lease Agreement
Closed-end Monthly Payments

Lease Date _____

Lessor:_____

Lease Arranger (if applicable): _____

Lessee:_____

DL#_____

State:_____Date DL issued:_____

Lessee:_____

DL#_____

State:_____Date DL issued:_____

1. **Description of Leased Vehicle:** ☐ New   ☐ Used

Make_____Year _____

Model_____Body Style _____

VIN No. _____Lic. No. (if known) _____

Beginning Mileage _____

Additional Description: _____

2. **Definitions:** "You," "your" and "Lessee" mean each person or legal entity, jointly and individually, who signs this Lease agreement as the "Lessee." "We," "our," "us" and "Lessor" mean the Lessor who signs this Lease agreement and its successors and assigns. The Lease Arranger, if one is identified above, helped arrange this Lease, but is not a party to the actual Lease contract. Disclosures in this Lease are made on behalf of the Lessor and any Lease Arranger.

3. **Agreement of Lease:** You agree to lease the motor vehicle described in section 1 ("Vehicle") from us according to the terms included on pages 1 and 2 of this lease agreement ("Lease"). The Federal Consumer Leasing Act Disclosures are also contract terms of this Lease agreement except for sections 7, 8(b) and 10 which are made for disclosure purposes only.

Federal Consumer Leasing Act Disclosures

4. **Amount Due at Lease Signing or Delivery** (Itemized Below)* $_____

5. **Monthly Payments**
    Your first Monthly Payment of $_____ is due on _____, followed by _____ payments of $_____ due on the _____ day of each month beginning _____. The total of your Monthly Payments is $_____.

6. **Other Charges** (not part of your Monthly Payment)
Disposition Fee (if you do not purchase the Vehicle)

$_____

_____   _____

_____   _____

Total   _____

7. **Total of Payments** (The amount you will have paid
by the end of the Lease) $_____

8. ***Itemization of Amount Due at Lease Signing or
Delivery**

(a) Amount Due At Lease Signing or Delivery:

   (1) Capitalized Cost Reduction $_____
   (2) First Monthly Payment   _____
   (3) Refundable Security Deposit   _____
   (4) Title fees   _____
   (5) Registration fees   _____
   (6) _____   _____
   (7) _____   _____
   (8) _____   _____
   (9)   Total   _____

(b) How the Amount Due at Lease Signing or Delivery Will Be Paid:

   (1) Net trade-in allowance $_____
   (2) Rebates and noncash credits   _____
   (3) Amount to be paid in cash   _____
   (4)   Total   _____

9. **Your Monthly Payment is Determined as Shown Below:**

(a) **Gross Capitalized Cost.** The agreed upon value of the Vehicle ($_____) and any items you pay over the Lease term (such as service contracts, insurance, and any outstanding prior credit or lease balance)

$_____

If you want an itemization of this amount, please initial here: X_____(Lessee initials)

(b) **Capitalized Cost Reduction.** The amount of any net trade-in allowance, rebate, noncash credit, or cash you pay that reduces the Gross Capitalized Cost

−_____

(c) **Adjusted Capitalized Cost.** The amount used in calculating your Base Monthly Payment

=_____

(d) **Residual Value.** The value of the Vehicle at the end of the Lease used in calculating your Base Monthly Payment

−_____

(e) **Depreciation And Any Amortized Amounts.** The amount charged for the Vehicle's decline in value through normal use and for other items paid over the Lease term

=_____

(f) **Rent Charge.** The amount charged in addition to the Depreciation And Any Amortized Amounts

+_____

(g) **Total of Base Monthly Payments.** The Depreciation And Any Amortized Amounts plus the Rent Charge

=_____

(h) **Lease Term.** The number of months in your Lease

÷_____

(i) **Base Monthly Payment.**   =_____

(j) **Monthly Sales/Use Tax.**   +_____

(k) _____   +_____

(l) _____   +_____

(m) **Total Monthly Payment.**   =$_____

10. Early Termination. You may have to pay a substantial charge if you end this Lease early. <u>The charge may be up to several thousand dollars.</u> The actual charge will depend on when the Lease is terminated. The earlier you end the Lease, the greater this charge is likely to be.

11. **Excessive Wear and Use.** You may be charged for excessive wear based on our standards for normal use and for mileage in excess of _____ miles per year at the rate of _____ per mile.

12. **Purchase Option at End of Lease Term.**

☐ You do not have an option to purchase the Vehicle at the end of the Lease term.

☐ You have an option to purchase the Vehicle at the end

of the Lease term for $_____ plus the following additional costs and fees: _____. This purchase option price does not include official fees such as for taxes, tags, licenses and registration, which you will also be required to pay.

13. **Other Important Terms.** See your Lease documents for additional information on early termination, purchase options and maintenance responsibilities, warranties, late and default charges, insurance, and any security interest, if applicable.

"e" means estimate

PA Notice: If you do not meet your contract obligations, you may lose the Vehicle and the right to use it under this Lease.

AK and SD Notice: If this Lease is for a consumer purpose, then this Lease is **CONSUMER PAPER.**

---

14. **DESCRIPTION OF TRADE-IN:** Make: _____ Year: _____ Model: _____ Outstanding Prior Credit or Lease Balance on Trade-In (if any) $_____.

15. **ESTIMATED OFFICIAL FEES AND TAXES. The total ESTIMATED amount you will pay for official license fees, registration title, and taxes over the entire term of the Lease, whether included with your Monthly Payments or assessed otherwise, is $_____.**

16. **ADDITIONAL FEES AND CHARGES:** In addition to the other amounts promised in this Lease, you agree to pay the following:

(a) SECURITY DEPOSIT: If included in the itemized Amount Due At Lease Signing or Delivery section (section 8(a)(3)), you will give us a refundable Security Deposit in the amount indicated. It may be used to pay any amount that you do not pay when due. After all your obligations are paid under this Lease, we will return any remaining amount to you. You will not be entitled to interest on your Security Deposit or to any other benefit, increase or profits that accrue to us as a result of holding the Security Deposit. No Security Deposit will be collected if this is a consumer-purpose Lease governed by the law of West Virginia.

(b) VEHICLE RETURN FEE: You will pay us a Vehicle Return fee of $_____ if this Lease is terminated before the end of the scheduled Lease term and the Vehicle is returned to us or to our agents. This Fee will not apply if the Lease ends early by your purchase of the Vehicle.

(c) DISPOSITION FEE: You will pay us a Disposition Fee of $_____ when you return the Vehicle at the end of the scheduled Lease term. This Fee will not apply if the Lease ends early or if you buy the Vehicle at the end of the Lease term (if you have that option).

(d) LATE CHARGE: Unless prohibited, you will pay us

a Late Charge of _____ for any Monthly Payment that is not paid in full within ___ days after it is due.

17. VOLUNTARY ADDITIONAL PROTEC-TIONS: You may buy any of the following VOLUN-TARY protection plans. They are NOT required as part of this Lease and will NOT be a factor in our decision to lease the Vehicle to you.

(a) SERVICE CONTRACT: You may, but are not required to, purchase a Service Contract to cover

_____.

The Service Contract will be in effect for _____ and will provide up to _____ of coverage. The coverage costs $_____.

Your signature below means you want the described Service Contract and that you received and reviewed a copy of it. If no coverage or price is given above, you have declined any such coverage that we offered.

LESSEE SIGNATURE	LESSEE SIGNATURE

(b) CREDIT INSURANCE: Credit life and credit dis-ability (accident and health or accident and sickness) insurance are NOT required as part of this Lease and will NOT be a factor in our decision to lease the Vehi-cle to you. If you want such insurance, we will obtain it for you (if you qualify for coverage). We are quoting below ONLY the coverages that you have chosen to purchase.

Credit Life: Insured _____

☐ Single   ☐ Joint   Prem. $_____   Term_____

Credit Disability: Insured _____

☐ Single   ☐ Joint   Prem. $_____   Term_____

Your signature below means you want (only) the insurance coverage(s) quoted above. If none are quoted, you have declined any coverages we offered.

LESSEE SIGNATURE	LESSEE SIGNATURE

(c) GAP WAIVER OR GAP COVERAGE: You are liable for the early termination charges in section 36 if this Lease ends early because the Vehicle is stolen and not recovered, or is lost or destroyed, or is damaged and we determine that it cannot or should not be repaired. On such termination, the amount of your insurance proceeds for the Vehicle may not be enough to pay the early termination charges. This difference is generally referred to as the "Gap" amount.

You may, but are not required to, purchase a Gap Waiver or Gap Coverage Contract ("Gap Product") to cover the "Gap" amount as it is specifically defined in the separate Gap Product. The Gap Product will be in effect for the entire scheduled Lease term and will provide up to _____
of coverage. The Gap Product costs $_____.

Your signature below means you want the described Gap Waiver or Coverage Contract and that you received and reviewed a copy of it. If no coverage or price is given above, you have declined any such coverage that we offered.

LESSEE SIGNATURE	LESSEE SIGNATURE

18. **WARRANTIES:** The Vehicle is subject to the following express warranties that apply to this Lease:

(a) The standard written manufacturer's warranty. This warranty is made by the manufacturer and NOT by the Lessor.

(b) _____

_____.

By signing this Lease you acknowledge receiving a copy of the above written warranties.

YOU UNDERSTAND THAT WE (THE LESSOR) MAKE NO EXPRESS OR IMPLIED WARRANTIES OTHER THAN THOSE DESCRIBED IN SUBSECTION (b) OF THIS SECTION (IF ANY). **EXCEPT AS REQUIRED BY LAW, LESSOR MAKES NO IMPLIED WARRANTY OF MERCHANTABILITY AND NO WARRANTY THAT THE VEHICLE IS FIT FOR A PARTICULAR PURPOSE.** Except as provided above, you will take the Vehicle **AS IS** and **WITH ALL FAULTS.** We do not exclude any warranties of merchantability and fitness for a particular purpose if: (a) this Lease is subject to Massachusetts law, or (b) this Lease is for a consumer or agricultural purpose and is subject to West Virginia law.

19. OPTION TO PURCHASE BEFORE THE END OF THE LEASE TERM.

You have the option to purchase the Vehicle any time after _____ months of this Lease as long as we have not declared the Lease to be in default. You must give us at least 30 days prior notice of your intent to purchase. The Vehicle sale price will be the sum of: (a) All officials' fees, taxes and other costs incurred for the purchase (or to prepare the Vehicle for purchase) and all other fees and charges then due or past due under the Lease; and (b) _____

_____.

20. OPTION TO PURCHASE AT THE END OF THE LEASE TERM: The Purchase Option at End of Lease Term section in the Federal Consumer Leasing Act Disclosures (section 12) describes your option to purchase the Vehicle at the end of the scheduled Lease term (if any) and the Vehicle's purchase price. If you have the option, it is available only if we have not already declared the Lease to be in default. You also must give us at least 30 days prior notice of your intent to purchase.

21. ASSIGNMENTS AND TRANSFERS: We may

sell, assign, or in any other way transfer our rights and responsibilities in the Vehicle and this Lease.

YOU WILL NOT SUBLEASE THE VEHICLE, ASSIGN, PLEDGE OR PERMIT A SECURITY INTEREST TO BE CREATED IN, OR IN ANY OTHER WAY TRANSFER YOUR INTERESTS OR RESPONSIBILITIES IN THE VEHICLE AND IN THIS LEASE. We may, at our discretion, give you permission to make a transfer that is otherwise prohibited. Such permission must be given in writing prior to any transfer.

22. **PRIMARY USE OF THE VEHICLE:** You intend to use the Vehicle **primarily** for personal, family or household purposes unless you initial below.

> LESSEE INITIALS

The Vehicle will be used **primarily** for business, commercial or agricultural purposes.

23. **ENTIRE AGREEMENT:** This Lease contract contains your and our entire agreement. There are no unwritten agreements regarding this Lease contract. Any change to this Lease contract must be in writing and signed by you and by us.

LESSEE SIGNATURE

LESSEE SIGNATURE

24. LESSEE SIGNATURE(S): YOU AGREE TO ALL THE PROVISIONS ON **PAGES 1 AND 2** OF THIS LEASE. YOU HAVE READ PAGES 1 AND 2 OF THIS LEASE AND ACKNOWLEDGE RECEIVING A COMPLETED COPY OF THIS LEASE.

Lessee:

✎ ✗   Date:

Title (business leases):

Lessee:

✎ ✗   Date:

Title (business leases):

25. **LESSOR SIGNATURE:** By signing below, Lessor agrees to the terms and conditions contained on pages 1 and 2 of this Lease and provides:

(a) Lessee DL Inspection. The Lessor inspected each Lessee's driver's license and compared and verified the signature on each license with a signature of each Lessee, written in Lessor's presence. Lessor believes that each Lessee providing such information is currently licensed to drive by the state of his/her residence.

(b) Assignment. Lessor assigns this Lease and all rights and title to the Vehicle to the Assignee identified below (if any):

Assignee Name: CUSTOMER IMPRINT

Address: (IMPRINT AREA D)

This assignment is subject to a separate Assignment Agreement between the Lessor and Assignee.

Lessor:

| ✎ ✗ | Date: |

Title:

Motor Vehicle Lease Agreement—Page 2

---

26. **GENERAL TERMS:** You agree that the law of the state where this contracts is signed will govern this Lease, unless prohibited. If any part of this Lease cannot be enforced, the rest of the Lease will still be enforceable.

27. **VEHICLE USE:** You agree: (a) to allow the Vehicle only to be operated only by licensed drivers for lawful purposes and in a lawful manner; (b) to operate the Vehicle only as recommended by the manufacturer; (c) not to use the Vehicle as a taxi or for other public or private hire or delivery; (d) not to use the Vehicle in a way that causes the cancellation or suspension of any warranty, insurance or other similar Vehicle protection agreement; (e) not to take the Vehicle out of the state where you reside for more than 30 consecutive days without our prior written approval; and (f) not to take the Vehicle out of the United States without our prior written approval.

28. MAINTENANCE AND OPERATING COSTS:

You agree to keep the Vehicle in the same condition as when you received it, except for reasonable wear and mileage. You agree to service and maintain it as recommended by the manufacturer and as needed to keep it in good operating condition. You also agree to maintain the Vehicle so that any warranties or similar agreements remain effective and so that it passes all inspections required by law. You are responsible for paying all costs of the Vehicle's service, repair and maintenance and all the costs of its operation, including the costs of gas, oil, parking and storage, etc. You agree to make the Vehicle available to us for inspection during the Lease term at any reasonable time and location that we request.

29. TITLING, OFFICIAL FEES AND TAXES: You

understand and agree that this agreement is a lease only. We own the Vehicle and it will be titled in our name or in the name of our assignee. You have no ownership interests in the Vehicle except for any future options to purchase provided in this Lease.

You agree to pay all title, registration, license, sales, use, excise, personal property, ad valorem, inspection, testing, and all other taxes, fees and charges imposed by government authorities in connection with the Vehicle and this Lease during the Lease term, except our income taxes. If such amounts are assessed for a period during the Lease term, you will pay them even if they become due after the Lease term. We may, at our discretion, determine the timing and procedures for payment of these amounts. You will promptly pay these amounts as they come due unless otherwise indicated in this Lease.

30. **REQUIRED INSURANCE:** You agree to provide at least the following insurance coverage ("Required Insurance") on the Vehicle at all times during this Lease: (a) LIABILITY for bodily injury or death of others in an amount of at least $100,000 per person and $300,000 per occurrence; (b) LIABILITY for property damage to others in an amount of at least $50,000; and (c) COLLISION and COMPREHENSIVE (including fire and theft coverage) with a deductible not to exceed $500. You agree to provide the insurance at your own expense with a duly licensed insurer of your choice who is reasonably acceptable to us. This insurance may be provided through existing policies that you own or control. You also agree to name us or our assignee as loss payee and additional insured. The insurance policy must provide for at least 10 days advance notice to us of any cancellation or other material change in coverage. At our request, you will promptly provide us with written proof of insurance. You will promptly contact us in writing if any of the insurance provider information changes. You authorize us to endorse your name on any check we receive for insurance proceeds.

NOTICE: Liability insurance coverage for bodily injury and motor vehicle damage caused to others is not included in this Lease.

31. DAMAGE TO THE VEHICLE AND INSUR-ANCE CLAIMS: You will notify us in writing immediately after any loss to person or property occurs involving the Vehicle in any way. You will also notify us in writing immediately upon receiving notice of any demand, claim, or suit involving the Vehicle in any way. You agree to fully cooperate with us and with your insurer in any investigation, suit or other action resulting from the use or control of the Vehicle.

You agree to repair or compensate us for any loss or damage to the Vehicle that occurs during this Lease. If the Vehicle is damaged, we will decide if it is repairable and if it should be repaired. If the Vehicle is repaired, you will apply to the costs of repair any insurance proceeds you receive for its loss or damage. You understand that you must pay for any loss or damage that is not paid by insurance proceeds. You also must keep making any payments as they come due during this Lease even if the Vehicle is damaged or unusable for a period of time. The THEFT, LOSS OR UNREPAIRABLE DAMAGE section describes what happens if we decide that the Vehicle cannot or should not be repaired.

32. THEFT, LOSS OR UNREPAIRABLE DAM-AGE: If the Vehicle is stolen and not recovered, or is lost or destroyed, or is damaged and we determine that it cannot or should not be repaired, then we will decide whether to continue or terminate this Lease. If it is continued, you agree to accept a reasonable substitute vehicle of similar value, condition, mileage and accessories to replace the original Vehicle. If we terminate the Lease under this section, the event will be treated as an early termination and you will be required to pay the amounts described in the EARLY TERMINATION section.

33. **DEFAULT:** You will be in default on this Lease if any one of the following occurs (except as prohibited by law):

(a) You fail to make any payment when it is due;

(b) You fail to perform any material obligation that you have undertaken in this Lease (which includes doing something you have agreed not to do);

(c) The Vehicle is seized, confiscated, or levied upon by legal or governmental process;

(d) You fail to provide the Required Insurance on the Vehicle or fail to provide proof of such coverage after we request it;

(e) Anything else happens that creates a default according to applicable law.

If this Lease is in default, we may exercise our remedies against any or all Lessees.

34. **REMEDIES:** If this Lease is in default, we may take any one or more of the following actions. If the law requires us to do so, we will give you notice and wait any period of time required before taking these actions. We may:

(a) Terminate this Lease and your rights to use the Vehicle;

(b) Take any reasonable action to correct your default or to prevent our loss (including, for example, purchasing insurance that you agreed to provide). Any amount we pay will be added to the amount you owe us and will be immediately due;

(c) Require you to return the Vehicle and any related records or make them available to us in a reasonable manner;

(d) Take back the Vehicle by legal process or self help, but in doing so, we may not breach the peace or violate the law;

(e) Use any other remedy available to us in this Lease or by law.

You agree that, subject to your right to recover such property, we may take possession of personal property left in or on the Vehicle and taken into possession as provided above.

You agree to repay us for any reasonable amounts we pay to correct or cover your default, unless prohibited by law. You also agree to reimburse us for any costs and expenses we incur in the Vehicle's return and disposition or resulting from early termination, unless prohibited by law. This amount includes, for example, our court costs and reasonable attorneys' fees. Your responsibility to pay for our attorneys' fees is subject to any limitations provided by the applicable state law. If this Lease is subject to Colorado law, the fee will not exceed 15% of the unpaid debt if the Lease is for consumer purposes, unless otherwise directed by the court. If this Lease is subject to Georgia law, the fees are recoverable up to 15% of the amount owing. If this Lease is subject to Ohio law, you will not be responsible to pay for our attorneys' fees. Other limitations may apply in other states.

By choosing any one or more of these remedies, we do not give up our right to use another remedy. By deciding not to use any remedy should this Lease be in default, we do not give up our right to use that remedy if the same kind of default happens again.

35. **LEASE TERMINATION:** This lease will end ("terminate") when one of the following events occurs, whichever happens first: (a) You choose to end the Lease early and return the Vehicle to us; (b) You choose to buy the Vehicle (if you have that option); (c) You return the Vehicle at the end of the scheduled Lease term; (d) We terminate the Lease because the Vehicle is stolen and not recovered, or is lost or destroyed, or is damaged and we determine that it cannot or should not be repaired or replaced; (e) We terminate the Lease due to your default. On termination, you will pay the amounts agreed in this Lease. **You are not entitled to keep the Vehicle past the**

end of the scheduled Lease term or the date of early termination without our prior consent.

36. **EARLY TERMINATION:** This section applies if the Lease terminates before the end of the scheduled Lease term. It does not apply if you choose to buy the Vehicle before the end of the scheduled Lease term. On early termination, you will return the Vehicle to us. You will deliver it to our address or to another reasonable location at our request.

(a) **Early Termination Liability.** On early termination, you agree to pay us:

    (1) A VEHICLE RETURN FEE, if any, given in section 16(b);

    (2) All accrued and unpaid amounts that are due or past due at that time (including amounts described in the REMEDIES section);

    (3) The amount by which the "Adjusted Lease Balance" is greater than the "Realized Value" of the Vehicle. (If the Realized Value is greater than the Adjusted Lease Balance, this amount will be applied as a credit toward your liability) and;

    (4) All official fees and taxes imposed in connection with the Lease termination.

(b) **Determining the Adjusted Lease Balance.** Your early termination liability under this section will be calculated using the "Adjusted Lease Balance." The Adjusted Lease Balance at the beginning of this Lease is equal to the Adjusted Capitalized Cost given in section 9(c). Assuming that all Base Monthly Payments (given in section 9(i)) are made on time and you keep all your other Lease obligations, the Base Monthly Payments will be applied to reduce the Adjusted Lease Balance so that at the end of the Lease term the Adjusted Lease Balance equals the Vehicle's Residual Value (given in section 9(d)).

Your Base Monthly Payment will be applied first to the Rent Charge which is earned and charged each month in a way that is similar to interest for loans. Section 9(f) gives the total Rent Charge that we will earn over the scheduled Lease term. We will earn the Rent Charge at a constant rate throughout the scheduled Lease term. We will calculate the amount of the Rent Charge earned each month by applying the applicable constant rate to the Adjusted Lease Balance. The remainder of your Base Monthly Payment (if any) will be applied each month to reduce the Adjusted Lease Balance.

Each month, the portion of the Rent Charge paid out of your Base Monthly Payment will be subtracted from the total Rent Charge to be earned over the scheduled Lease term (section 9(f)). The difference is the "unearned" Rent Charge at that time.

At any given time, the Adjusted Lease Balance is equal to: (1) the Vehicle's Residual Value (given in section 9(d)), plus (2) the total of all remaining unpaid Base Monthly Payments, minus (3) the amount of the unearned Rent Charge at that time.

(c) **Determining the Realized Value.** If the law so requires, we will send you a notice and wait any required period of time before taking action to establish the Vehicle's Realized Value. Unless otherwise required by law, the Realized Value will be determined in one of the following ways: (1) by a written agreement between you and us reached within 15 days of the Vehicle's return; (2) by the professional appraisal of an independent third party agreed to by you and us and obtained at your expense within 15 days of the Vehicle's return (or a longer period, if all parties so agree or if the law so requires). The appraisal shall be of the Vehicle's wholesale value and shall be final and binding on both you and us; or (3) if it is not determined within 15 days of the Vehicle's return, we will determine the Realized Value in accordance with accepted practices in the automobile industry for determining the wholesale value of used vehicles by obtaining a wholesale cash bid for the purchase of the Vehicle or by disposing of the Vehicle in an otherwise commercially reasonable manner. If a bid procedure is used, you may have the right to submit a cash bid which we will consider along with any other offers we may receive. We do not have to sell the Vehicle but will use the highest offer amount we receive in calculating your liability. The Realized Value will be zero if the Vehicle is not returned to us. If this Lease is governed by Nevada law, you may submit to us a written bid for the purchase of the Vehicle at any time before we establish its Realized Value.

37. **SCHEDULED TERMINATION:** Unless this Lease ends under another section of this agreement, you will return the Vehicle to us on the last day of the scheduled Lease term. You agree to return it to our address or to another reasonable location that we may request. You may return the Vehicle up to 15 days before the last day of the scheduled Lease term at your option and for your own convenience, without any adjustment (charges or credits) for an "early" return.

On termination under this section, you agree to pay us:

(a) A DISPOSITION FEE, if any, described in section 16(c);

(b) An EXCESS WEAR CHARGE and a charge for excess mileage, if any, described in the EXCESS WEAR AND MILEAGE section; and

(c) All other amounts then due or past due under this Lease.

These amounts are due and payable at the time you return the Vehicle or as soon thereafter that they can be determined. You will also pay us for all reasonable losses and expenses we incur if you fail to return the Vehicle at the end of the scheduled Lease term.

38. **EXCESS WEAR AND MILEAGE:** When you return the Vehicle at the end of the scheduled Lease term, you agree to pay an EXCESS WEAR CHARGE for any excessive wear to the Vehicle. The EXCESS WEAR CHARGE will be equal to the actual or estimated costs of repair, or the estimated loss in its value, because of any excessive wear (even if we do not repair the Vehicle).

Excessive wear includes the repair or replacement of:

(a) **mechanical** damage, failure or defect, (b) **exterior** parts, grilles, bumpers, trim, paint and glass that are dented, scratched, chipped, discolored, or otherwise damaged, missing or worn beyond ordinary use, (c) **interior** parts, upholstery, dashboard, carpeting, or trunk liner that are stained, torn, burned or otherwise damaged, missing or worn beyond ordinary use, (d) **accessories, tools and equipment** included with the Vehicle when delivered that are missing, damaged or not in proper working order; (e) **tires** that are unsafe, have less than 1/8 inch tread at the shallowest point, or are not a part of a matching set of four, (f) any other part or condition that causes the Vehicle to be **unsafe or unlawful** to use, (g) any other damage or worn item(s) that together cost more than $50 to repair or replace.

We will notify you of the amount of these charges and provide any other related information as may be required by law. The charges will be due as soon as the amount is determined. If this Lease is subject to Connecticut law, the amount of these charges will be determined using the procedure required in Connecticut Public Law 95-337.

When you return the Vehicle at the end of the scheduled Lease term, you agree to pay any charge for excess mileage as described in section 11, Excessive Wear and Use.

39. **INDEMNITY:** To the fullest extent permitted by law, you agree to indemnify and hold us harmless and our successors and assigns from all liability, claims, losses, demands, damages of all kinds, expenses (including reasonable legal fees and expenses), fines and penalties we suffer or incur resulting from the possession, operation, condition, maintenance or use of the Vehicle during the Lease term.

40. **NOTICES:** Unless otherwise required by law, you agree that any notice we provide you will be reasonable and sufficient if it is sent by first class mail, addressed to you at the address given in this Lease or to your last known address as reflected in our records. You will notify us in writing within 30 days of any change in your address.

Glossary

"A" tier rate A more attractive interest rate, based on a consumer's good credit history

Accelerated depreciation Rate at which leasing companies are allowed by the government to depreciate a vehicle—faster than market depreciation

Acquisition fee The fee a leasing company charges up front to cover such costs as the credit check, documentation, and paperwork. Similar to the points a bank charges on a home mortgage

Actuarial formula Method of figuring a payoff using simple interest

Advanced Payment Plan Ford Motor Company's one-payment lease

Alternative financing A method of financing a vehicle to meet your transportation needs

Balance sheet The difference between assets and liabilities that determines a consumer's net worth

Bottom line A lease/buy comparison that weighs the down payment + loan payments against the residual + lease payments. Invalid, because the buy example is based on cash flow, and the lease example is based on expenses

Bump To increase the amount allowed on a trade-in

Buried in the trade Caught in a situation in which the trade-in is worth less then the payoff on the loan or lease

"C" or "D" tier rate Higher interest rate, based on a consumer's less-than-perfect credit history

Cap cost Capitalized cost. The price a leasing company pays for a vehicle, plus any additional costs

Cap-cost reduction Amount of money a customer pays up front to reduce capitalized cost and lower the lease payment

Capitalize To set an item up in your books as an asset

Captive finance company Finance company closely associated with a manufacturer. The three largest are GMAC, Ford Motor Credit, and Chrysler Credit. Most imports also have captive finance companies

Cash flow example Cash paid to purchase a vehicle—without considering its depreciation

Closed-end lease Lease at the end of which the customer can walk away without further obligation (assuming he has not exceeded the mileage allowance and the car has not been abused). Under this provision, the customer carries no risk for the future market value of the car

Commissionable gross The part of profit from which the salesperson's commission is taken

Cost of a vehicle The value a consumer gets for his money in acquiring a vehicle

CSI Customer Service Index—the rating dealers and salespersons receive from automobile manufacturers

Customer retention Percentage of current customers who return to the same dealer or leasing company for their next vehicle

De-cap Another term for cap-cost reduction

Deficiency The difference between the payoff on a car before its lease is up and the actual cash value of the vehicle; the amount the customer must pay to terminate the lease early

Depreciation The dollar amount that a vehicle loses in market value during use

Disclosure Information that is now required by law to appear on all leases

Disposition fee A fee paid to the leasing company if a vehicle is returned at the end of the lease

Drive-away fees Fees that a customer pays up front. These may include a security deposit, the first month's payment, and license and title fees

Educational process Explanation to a customer of all features of leasing

Equity Difference between the value of an item and the amount owed on it

Expense example A lease calculation based on a vehicle's depreciation

Fair market residual Option allowing a lease customer to purchase his vehicle at the end of the lease for an unspecified amount. Value will be determined at the end of the lease, not up front

Federal Truth in Leasing Act Regulation M New law, effective January 1, 1998

Financial inversion Politically correct term (see **Buried in the trade**) for the situation of a customer who owes more on his trade-in than the vehicle is worth

GAP protection An insurance policy covering the difference between a settlement from an insurance company and the actual payoff on a vehicle that has been stolen or totaled

ITC Investment tax credit

Lease charges The lease rate plus other fees. See also **Acquisition fee, Disposition fee.**

Lease rate Charges added to a lease to cover the economic use value of an asset (similar to interest)

Leasing A less expensive way to get the make and model you want in a new vehicle. Leases usually run for two to four years

Leasing penetration The leasing percentage of total retail deliveries. A dealer who delivers 100 cars a month and leases 25 of them has a 25% leasing penetration

Lessee An individual who leases a vehicle for personal use

Lessor The company that owns a leased vehicle

Leverage Maximum use of an asset

Money factor A shortcut method of figuring lease charges. It converts interest rates

Monthly obligation ratio A formula for measuring monthly income against monthly obligations; used to determine whether a consumer qualifies for a loan or a lease

MSRP Manufacturer's suggested retail price

Negative equity Condition of owing more on a trade-in than the vehicle is worth

Net lease Another term for closed-end or walk-away lease

Off-balance-sheet financing Obligations that are not reflected in a consumer's net worth on a balance sheet. Leasing is an example of off-balance-sheet financing. Lease obligations do appear on credit reports and sometimes as notes on a balance sheet

One-payment lease A conventional lease with one payment made up front (the total of monthly lease payments minus interest). Also called a **Single-payment lease**

Open-end lease Lease agreement whereby the customer shares in the vehicle's ultimate resale value at the end of the lease. If the car sells for more than the guaranteed residual, the customer profits. If it sells for less, the customer takes the loss

Option to buy Lease provision allowing the customer to purchase the vehicle when the lease is up. Lets the customer know up front how much he will have to pay for the car at the end

Over advance Additional amount paid to the dealer by the leasing company to help a customer with negative equity. Makes funds available to pay the lien holder the difference between the value of the trade-in and the actual payoff

Price of a vehicle What the customer pays for the vehicle

Rebates Cash subsidies that manufacturers offer on certain makes and models

Regulation M Leasing legislation first passed in 1976. Updated effective January 1, 1998. See **Federal Truth in Leasing Act**

Renting Expensive arrangement through which a customer can drive a used vehicle for a short period of time—a day, week, or month—with no option to buy

Residual value Amount for which a lease company predicts a vehicle will sell at the end of a lease. Used to calculate lease payment

"Rule of 78s" Formula used to calculate the payoff if a lease is terminated early. It applies more of past payments to interest, less to principal reduction

Security deposit Payment made at the beginning of a lease, refundable if customer has adhered to the terms of the lease

Single-payment lease See **One-payment lease**

Smart/Lease Plus GMAC's one-payment—or single-payment—lease plan

Start-up fee Money a customer pays up front to start a lease. Most of this fee is a cap-cost reduction, but it also includes license, title, and taxes in some states

Subsidized leases Leases on certain makes and models through which manufacturers offset lease charges and raise vehicles' residuals in order to lower monthly payments and attract consumers

Subvented residual A type of manufacturer's subsidy through which the residual on certain vehicles is raised in order to lower monthly lease payments and make the vehicles more affordable

Sum of the digits See **"Rule of 78s"**

Term The number of months in a lease contract

TRAC lease Terminal rental adjustment clause —IRS terminology for an open-end lease

Trade cycle The number of years a customer keeps a vehicle before trading it in. The current average is 37 months

"24 Rule" The formula used to convert a Lease Charge Percentage to a Money Factor, or a Money Factor to a Lease Charge Percentage

Upside-down in their trade See **Buried in the trade; Financial inversion**

Walk-away lease See **Closed-end lease**

Write-off A tax-deductible expense; to deduct an expense from one's taxes